The JESUS PAPERS

The JESUS PAPERS

BISHOP JAMES I. YOUNG

Copyright © 2015 by Bishop James I. Young.

Library of Congress Control Number:		2015901560
ISBN:	Hardcover	978-1-5035-3977-8
	Softcover	978-1-5035-3978-5
	eBook	978-1-5035-3979-2

All rights reserved. No part of this book may be reproduced or transmitted in any form or by any means, electronic or mechanical, including photocopying, recording, or by any information storage and retrieval system, without permission in writing from the copyright owner.

Any people depicted in stock imagery provided by Thinkstock are models, and such images are being used for illustrative purposes only.
Certain stock imagery © Thinkstock.

This book was printed in the United States of America.

Scripture quotations marked KJV are from the Holy Bible, King James Version (Authorized Version). First published in 1611. Quoted from the KJV Classic Reference Bible, Copyright © 1983 by The Zondervan Corporation.

Rev. date: 01/30/2015

To order additional copies of this book, contact:
Xlibris
1-888-795-4274
www.Xlibris.com
Orders@Xlibris.com
700764

Part I

Moving Jesus beyond the two fish and five loaves of bread,
beyond the wine at the wedding,
beyond the raising of Lazarus from the dead,
and beyond just walking on the Sea of Galilee.

But blessed are your eyes, for they see, and your ears, for they hear.
—Matthew 13:16

CONTENTS

Introduction
-[9]-

The New Testament Jesus
-[13]-

The Truthful Realization of Jesus
-[35]-

The Brilliant Teachings of Jesus
-[37]-

Jesus
-[49]-

Wave Interference
-[51]-

The Works of Jesus
-[52]-

Even Greater Works
-[76]-

The Virtue of Jesus
-[88]-

True Believers of the True Works
-[95]-

The True and Living God
-[100]-

The Spirit of Truth
-[105]-

INTRODUCTION

IN PSALM 97:11, LIGHT is sown for the righteous, and as children of light (John 12:36) and the light of the world (Matt. 5:14), we believe in the light while we have light, and we believe that rearranging the spectrum of light means altering the velocity of light. Rearranging the colors in a light wave means rearranging the speeds of that light wave.

The seven spectrums of a light wave reveal the seven speeds of natural light, and the light wave cannot be altered to formulate two reds or two greens or two oranges or two yellows coexisting side by side because the wave of light exhibits only its seven spectrums, and should any of these seven spectrums be altered in this wave packet, then the velocity of that wave packet and beam temperature would be changed. Therefore, light and the speed of light is relative to these seven spectrums of the wave packet and beam temperature. In nature, the wave packet has already been formed to make the present speed for light relative to any such observer of that spectrum.

We believe that in its present wave packet and form and intensity, the speed of light is determined in nature for that composite spectrum of light shown to the observer and that it is relative to the observer of that composite spectrum of light. Other than being altered in the present composite spectrum for the formulation for varying speeds of light, that is, altering the blue spectrum in the wave packet to the place of the red spectrum in the wave packet for infrablue or any of the other seven wave spectrums. When altering them into their infrazones, if the composite wave spectrum of the present wave structure were doubled so that the whole wave packet would be red beside red, blue beside blue, green beside green, orange beside orange, and that this was the composite spectrum for the whole packet wave for light, then the super speed or the super velocity of light ought to occur, causing the velocity and intensity of light to intensify and travel twelve trillion miles (12,000,000,000,000) in one year and that the super speed or super velocity of light would remain super relative to any observer.

The lengthening or the shortening of the spectrums of the wave packet, whether all spectrums of the wave packet are uniformly long or short in length within the wave packet itself, would also cause a variation and if not a variation of its velocity, then a variation of its gravitational effects, if not also of its luminosity. A double and parallel red spectrum, a double and parallel blue spectrum, or a double and parallel violet spectrum would increase the luminosity of the wave packet, and that is if the double and parallel wave packet is of a uniform spectrum for all color spectrums within the wave packet. This does not imply a shift in any direction for any double parallel color spectrum within the parallel wave packet. That is, any color spectrum is not shifted longer or shortened, nor are they separated, one red from another red within the wave packet.

The law of nature has simplified the wave packet and spectrum by limiting the spectrum to seven within a wave packet. In keeping with the natural law of compliance, the theoretical intellect can lengthen or shorten these set elements within the wave spectrum of natural light. There have been found variations and higher intensities in some light emissions, moving the present standard for the single wave packet spectrum into higher realms of emissions for light.

Within regions and realms of high energy cosmic space where matter is compact and spectrums of light are released by massive explosions, releasing fascinating intensities of cosmic energies, problems could occur with the speed and spectrum of a wave packet of light in or near an earthly atmosphere of the present sort.

Taking nature to realms higher and away from an earthly atmosphere of the present sort to where her forces become unified, a difference in the present spectrum and the natural measurements of laws, would also show variations from a unified nature. This would indeed prove incredible to some. But to children of light, your duty is to see beyond such things.

Most of those who experiment with light do not believe in the living God, but Jesus spoke to those who do and believe in such that they may be the children of light, so why should nonbelievers be wiser than you?

THE NEW TESTAMENT JESUS

THE JESUS WE ARE about to introduce to the church and the world seem not to be known fully by either the church or the world. Indeed, He was in the world, and the world was made by Him, and the world knew Him not. Now what does it mean by He was in the world? If we put this very knowledge at the very edge of our understanding to comprehend how it is that He who made the world was in the world and had to be some part within the world, then we can understand why he had to be in the world, which He himself made. Of how important it is for you to know that He was within the world, whereas there can be no doubt that He made a shell of a world without considering its internal and working parts and habitations. We, therefore, must need to know that He was in the world.

Now the internal materials comprising the advent of Him within the world and its workings before and even while He is within the world constitutes another field of knowledge, which the church does not address at all. The definition of the word given here for the world is the cosmos, and truly, how many from the church virtually define the world to mean the cosmos? When you now consider that He was in the cosmos and the cosmos was made by Him, and the cosmos knew Him not, the question is when and where did the cosmos go dead? That is, if He who made the cosmos is alive within it; if the cosmos knew Him not either before now or then at His present, why would the very cosmos not be alive at the advent of its living maker? At some point, it must have died, for it knew Him not that liveth, who made it. Now the question is this: Can those who live within the cosmos and under the cosmos live even though the cosmos may be proven dead? First, consider how vast the cosmos is by comparing it to your minute mass and size within it. The very presence of Jesus, even here on earth, proved that you could live within and under a dead cosmos. As proof of this, by the very words of Jesus himself, He said, "I am come that they might have life, and that they might have it more abundantly" (John 10:10). Though the cosmos knew Him not, being dead and desolate.

There are some among you who may not find the cosmos desolate, being filled with so much astrophysical and cosmic matter. I know that you have charted the heavens and come away with vicissitudes of star fields and cosmic working orders, but they are all dead creatures, if they live not according to Christ. When He who liveth cometh, all of them shall flee away at His coming. Amen.

Now before we produce the unheard of about the Jesus from the New Testament, those other books claiming to know Jesus, which are not of the New Testament, reveal nothing more than the New Testament writers and the New Testament learners. Those of the church have not yet applied nowhere near the fullness of Jesus, even though, of His fullness have we all received, and grace for grace. Now what does that mean? Of His fullness have all we received, and grace for grace? If He is full of life, you also are full of life. If you are full of grace and truth, it is because you have received it in its fullness from Him in the exact measure that He himself possesses, grace for grace. How many sin and fall short of this? Does this mean that you are a false Christ according to Matthew 24:24? Not at all because there shall arise false christs and false prophets, and they shall arise by their own choosing and power of falsehood and deception. What then of His fullness have all we received, and grace for grace? Having then received it from Him, as opposed to having it arise through falsehood and deception, will prove truth worth in great signs and wonders. These signs and wonders are simply of the world order to deceive those ignorant of His fullness given to us to receive. Simply because those of His church have not known to receive of His fullness, even grace for grace, has given cause for these falsehood deceivers to arise, robbing them of their rightful powers to convert souls. Instead, those souls, which ought to be converted to Christ by the proper usage of these powers are used, therefore, to deceive the lost souls, to lead them away into destruction and everlasting punishment away from Christ, who is ready to save them.

The world would not have you understand fully the new testament of Jesus because I testify of it that the works thereof are evil, He said in John 7:7. Not only that! Even when the comforter is come, He will reprove the world of sin and of righteousness, and of judgment (John 16:8). But even with all of this He said, "For I came not to judge the world, but to save the world" (John 12:47), although the world would not have you understand fully the New Testament Jesus.

Now I would have you consider a very small strip and interval of time. Not the three hundred years that Enoch walked with God (Gen. 5:22), nor the one hundred and twenty years it took Noah to construct His ark (Gen. 6:3), nor the four hundred years of Israel's sojourning in Egyptian bondage (Gen. 15:13), nor the forty of wandering in the wilderness (Deut. 1:3); but even a much smaller interval of time: about the time interval Isaiah hath walked naked and barefoot (Isa. 20:3), three years. Within a mere three-year interval of time, what are some of the things that Jesus did even without paralleling the gospel? Although within the gospels we know of variations of things that He did, how is the church going to see those things written in the gospels in the magnificence of Him? I say, glory for glory, so many more things of the New Testament Jesus are lost to the understanding of the saints. Are we overreading the gospels in our understanding of the New Testament

Jesus? No. But on the contrary, the understanding of the New Testament Jesus is being underread by both the church and the world.

Take the ancient writing of some of the ancient easterners who performed some of those miracles that Jesus did hundreds of years before His earthly birth. Some of these ancient easterners were before Abraham, according to their written and ancient histories, which recorded some of their acts of wonder. But we are not here to glorify anyone else but one Christ Jesus, and understand what the New Testament revealed of Him in just three short years of His ministry, beginning with the very day that John baptized Him to begin His miraculous acts to the day He began His ministry as a man among men. Any other act following that day of His baptism would mount up to heaven, just as He did on the day He was baptized. But I perceive that the Lord has mingled a perverse spirit in the midst of the people so that they could not clearly see the many acts of Jesus without perverseness from the New Testament writings, which remain unto this very day.

Let us take into consideration the very day when Jesus was baptized by John, when He came from Galilee to the Jordan. If I am a liberal, I devise liberal things, and by liberal things, I shall stand (Isa. 32:8). I did not devise the baptism of Jesus by John in the Jordan, but I do abide by the liberal understanding of the proper interpretation of scripture, in what and how it declares about Jesus in the New Testament. Having read so many commentaries about the event, which ushered in Jesus's ministry of how, when He was baptized that day, He walked out of the water onto the bank of Jordan. Being shown something much more miraculous than this spectacular event that day, I decided to become more amazed at that day and moment fit only for the Savior of the world. If you do not understand that moment of His manifestation to Israel and of why He was manifested that miraculous way on that day, you may never understand why John baptized Him at all.

John himself said he baptized Jesus to make Him manifest to Israel (John 1:31). Therefore, there had to be an act of manifestation to Israel.

How was this act of manifestation to occur? Not by an ordinary action. The manifestation of the Redeemer of the world must be spectacular and beholding. No amount of sunlight nor ignorance will dare dim such a moment of splendor, and without a doubt, John said, "Therefore am I come baptizing with water, that He should be made manifest to Israel." The key word here is manifest. To cause to be made spectacular, when at the baptizing of water or do you think that fulfilling all righteousness does not require the miraculous? (Matt. 3:15). Being made manifest to all Israel means that all the righteousness before all of Israel is manifested in full before them. Being made manifest in full before them requires a magnificent moment before them. Now maybe the lowly and carnal mind of man is able to view this great moment, which the greatest ministry the world would ever know is manifested. If you cannot grasp this initial manifestation on the Jordan, how then can you grasp other and greater manifestations of Him from the New Testament?

Please read the verse of the moment of this manifestation of the Savior of the world to Israel very carefully and take time to study it prayerfully. If my interpretation of this manifestation is found to be wrong, I ask for your forgiveness. Nevertheless, I will not change it before the Lord himself.

Here, therefore, is that manifestation: And Jesus, when he was baptized, went up, straightway, out of the water (Matt. 3:16). Straightway, he went up, out of the water, standing upright out of the water, like a rocket launched from its pad. The next description is the best description that Matthew can give. And lo, the heavens were opened unto Him. He was received into the heavens, from the Jordan. He did not get baptized and then walk from the river to the shore. The grand manifestation even shook the writer Matthew: "And lo, the heavens were opened unto Him."

There are greater things to be more amazed at about the Lord. Some would find it difficult to see the Lord Jesus suspended within the heavens over Jordan, yet these same people would preach, with God, all things are possible (Matt. 19:26).

Now that baptism being the beginning run of His three-year ministry, those miracles, which are recorded within that three-year run of His ministry, are dwarfed by greater revelations in His ministry.

John bore witness of Him, but how do you bear witness of Him? Is your witness of Him true? Yet the New Testament gospel gives us a higher understanding of Jesus. An understanding so high up of Him that those things which we read of Him in the gospel in the three years of His ministry beginning from the baptism and manifestation would render the human mind in acceptance of them, null and void in their magnificence and brilliance. Those of the church are aptly able to grasp the full truth of those miracles of scripture and beyond the New Testament writings of Him. Greater magnitudes of Him still exist that stagger their revelations of Him.

Would anyone straightway leave their nets and follow Jesus without observing some great manifestation of Him? (Matt. 4:20). Would anyone immediately leave their ship and their father and their nets without first being affected by some great and overwhelming manifestation? (Matt. 4:22)

The unwritten magnitudes of Jesus just continue to grow and grow over these things already written in the gospels but are not written in other books properly transcribed from eyewitness accounts of Him. Though they may not be rightly divided in truthfulness, within the three years of His ministry, there are some who just believe Him the very best that they can.

To this point, Jesus declared, "Blessed are they that have not seen, and yet have believed" (John 20:29). We do get great variations away from those signs and works, which Jesus did in the gospels, but you may ask, how can that be that great variations away from those of the gospel may be obtained? Simply because we believe Jesus to be bigger than the gospels reveal about Himself, and that due to their limited ability, they could only reveal so much about the acts, the signs, the wonders and the works of the Lord himself. And if the Lord is greater than the temple (Matt. 12:6); greater than Jonas (Matt. 12:41); and greater than Solomon (Matt. 12:42), and proved himself also greater than the enemy (Matt. 4:11), should He not be greater than their writings about Him? The New Testament gospels, although inspired, wrote what they themselves could only know about Him. And they, although inspired by God, could only write of their own personal amazements of Him, often finding it difficult to describe just some of the signs and wonders of Jesus, as they actually had occasion to witness them.

How difficult it is to write and record the Messiah and Redeemer of the whole world soberly, with so many acts of amazements flooding the environment of those around Him, even as He performed wonders upon many of them. And consider the writings of those about Him, many hundreds of years before Him (John 12:41) and (John 5:46) even further back in the history before the New Testament gospels, or even further back in the claim of human history written before the writings in Moses's days (John 8:58), or to go even further back before the very day of Adam upon the earth (Isa. 43:13). How can you write fully of such a Messiah? But he cleared all of that up for the living writers of the gospels who needed not only inspiration but also lineage with Him in (Matt. 26:28).

When the time has fully come, when Jesus began His ministry at the age of thirty, the time set like the time for Bar Mitzvah (13), as like the number set for Jewish prayer (10), the Redeemer of the whole world for sin who was to fulfill all righteousness and come in the volume of the book (Ps. 40:7), as it is written of himself, was not to make any less a triumphant entry at the introduction of His ministry than He made upon His triumphant entry into Jerusalem at the close of His ministry (Matt. 21:8–9), nor of his birth thirty years earlier (Matt. 2:1), and for some who has shortsightedness about the early childhood of Jesus from the Bible, after His birth and visits of shepherds and wise men from the east. The great stir within Herod's temple or the wise Simeon or Anna at His purification is very apparent that the year before His Bar Mitzvah, he accompanied His parents to Jerusalem at their Passover pilgrimage (Luke 2:41).

There need not be guesswork about the life of the earlier childhood of Jesus, even before He reached the year before His Bar Mitzvah in Nazareth of Galilee. Now with so much having occurred even after those things of His birth, the star and magi, the shepherds and the angels, before Simeon and Anna and even after Simeon's eighth-day prediction of Him, this child is godsend and is set for the fall and rising again of many in Israel (Luke 2:34) at His purification or the parallel prophetic fulfillment of the daughter of Phanuel (Luke 2:38).

With so many things occurring in the youthful life of Jesus, even before He reached the presence of the scribes and wise men in the temple, astounding their understanding as a child, not even yet Bar Mitzvah age. It would do well for the readers to hear how such an astounding event at Jerusalem had been godly prepared in His own city of Nazareth.

Jesus had not yet reached the age that He was allowed to read any portion of the weekly Sedra, which divided the Torah into fifty-two equal portions for a yearly finish. He was not allowed to read the Torah until he would reach the age of Bar Mitzvah. Now any Jewish male having reached the proper age to become a man was then allowed to read that portion of the Sedra for the corresponding week of scripture, his thirteenth birthday having fallen within that period. He was then allowed to read that portion of the Sedra on the Sabbath day before the congregation, provided he had proven himself worthy at his own private Bar Mitzvah on a Thursday. Usually he is tutored in the reading of this portion of the Sedra by a rabbi at the request of his parents. Also during this time, the young Hebrew scholar would learn at a yeshiva (a place of learning). During the early days of Jesus, if you were taught in any other place outside Jerusalem itself, you were not customarily considered properly learned in Jewish law (see John 7:41, John 1:46, or John 7:15). Jesus did not attend the learning institutions or yeshiva at Jerusalem, but if you wish to know more about that portion of the proper childhood of Jesus, before we reveal so much more from the Bible, simply look away from the city of Jerusalem and its learning centers, the least of the two major cities during Jesus's upbringing toward the city of Nazareth, to hear what scripture has to say about His youthful learning before He astounded those at Jerusalem (Luke 2:40).

There are also other things about why He was able to astound those in the temple at Jerusalem at the age of twelve (Luke 2:4), one year before His Bar Mitzvah. Those who were taught at the schools and institutions at Jerusalem, those who became doctors of the law, scribes, and the priestly cast, and even of those who became lawyers and master Pharisees had no dealing with any knowledge other than the Sedra of the Torah, the Pentateuch, and the five books of Moses. It is clear from scripture that those of the synagogue of Nazareth had adopted the Haftorah. That is, along with the Sedra, they had also adopted the reading of portions of the prophets. Scripture would prove this in the later years of Jesus, when He would begin His ministry at the age of thirty after His baptism by John in the Jordan River (Luke 4:17), whereas at Jerusalem, only the Torah and Sedra were taught. While in the schools and synagogue of Nazareth, the Torah, the Sedra, the Psalms, and the Haftorah were taught and practiced among their youth, Jesus being one of them.

Now when it was time for Jesus's Bar Mitzvah at the synagogue of Nazareth, which had a different practice than those of Jerusalem, news had gone throughout Nazareth that one year earlier, at the age of twelve and while at the Holy Temple, sitting among doctors and scribes of the law (Luke 2:46), Jesus had caused amazement among them there. Now it was time for the child of wonder to become a man at the reading of the weekly Sedra and Haftora in the synagogue of Nazareth, which He visited each Sabbath day.

Since Jesus came in the volume of the book, it did not matter what portion of the Torah His Bar Mitzvah occurred in, whether in the beginning (Parshas Bereishis) or in the end of the Torah (Parshas V'zos Ha'Brochos). Unlike the schools of Jerusalem and among the Pharisee masters, who on the very day, completing V'zos Ha'Brochos, the cycle is renewed with Parshas Bereishis, to commence without the addition of the Haftorah. In this application of the Haftorah, the schools around Nazareth were different from those around Jerusalem, although those around Jerusalem were more noted in popularity. You should note that the grace of God was upon the growing up of Jesus (Luke 2:40); therefore, when the time of His Bar Mitzvah arrived at the age of thirteen, when Jesus became a man according to Jewish custom, this moment of His public fame would only be overshadowed by the public revelation of His timely ministry later (Luke 4:14) when He was about to begin His public ministry.

Knowing the approximate date of His birth would also give the approximate time of His Bar Mitzvah, which would also give the approximate Sedra of that week of His Bar Mitzvah, of which He would read publicly had he waited until the Sabbath to stand and read before the congregation at the synagogue of Nazareth. This would not have occurred on a Thursday, although he could have read a Parshas on Thursday in preparation for the Sabbath reading.

It is obvious from scriptures that on the day He became a man at His Bar Mitzvah reading, he greatly impacted those at the synagogue of Nazareth, At least to the extent that He was urged so often to read from the Torah even after His Bar Mitzvah, that He became a customary reader at the hometown synagogue at Nazareth. Little did those who heard Him read realize that they themselves would also become amazed at His reading when the time arrived about Him and His public ministry. The boy who would begin studying at five, would astound doctors at twelve years old, would put on phylacteries to recite

Torah at His Bar Mitzvah and thereafter would astound His hometown at thirty to begin His miraculous ministry.

How is it that He astounded so many as a child then but seems to have no effect upon the world now? The world seems to see Him as just an ordinary messiah doing just a few extraordinary things. I beg to differ with the world. Nay, I oppose the world's view in this paper for their misunderstanding and unacceptance of Him.

This is not a new gospel of Jesus Christ. There is none, nor is there any other Jesus nor Christ but one. It is now time to uncover Him, the likes of which has not been seen, save only a few recorded wonders of the gospels.

At the beginning of His public ministry, time is fulfilled (Mark 1:15). All righteousness is fulfilled (Matt. 3:15). He is here in the volume of the book (Heb. 10:7) a mere glance into these three advents alone to begin His public ministry, looking into those wonders already recorded within the Bible from time past ought to be enough to raise the understanding of any believer of the great magnitudes of following signs and wonders that should be done by Him in a continuous trend to the completion of His public ministry. The world, nor those of the church, is giving Jesus His full and true glorification, either because of ignorance or misunderstanding of His acts of divinity doing the three short years of His public ministry. That three-year period of time on earth is the most incredible time period of any other act or event in the history of the world. No other period of time nor acts or events could approach its magnificence of signs and wonders among mankind upon earth. When the fullness of time is present, any possible thing or act of time is available during that fullness of time. And likewise, during the fulfilling of all righteousness, any and all possible things of righteousness are able to be done in truth. When you come in the volume of the Holy Bible, the living creator of that Holy Bible makes available to the recipient of that holy book any and everything available written therein. Here, that recipient is Jesus (Luke 24:27).

Those things concerning him, according to all scriptures, would indeed not only fill all scripture but since He came in the volume of the book, they would also fulfill all scriptures. All of these written things concerning himself cannot be known by frail, doubting, and unbelieving minds without vision and acceptance of Him in the book.

Were you to draw a circle and perforate some point on that circle to cause that particular perforated point to stand out, then you may grasp the distinction of that three-year period of the public ministry of Jesus by the perforation and distinction with other events of time. Why do I use this illustration of a circle? Because the word galilee means circle, and within that interval of time, Jesus did things that the writers of the gospels could only grasp partially.

He could convey Himself away at will while vast multitudes watched in awe and amazement. He would levitate Himself at will when necessity prompted Him to do so. He would change His form to meet present conditions. He would vanish into the winds at will. He would also vanish into thin air at the change of attitude. He would change weather conditions to suit His own comfort. Sometimes He would outshine the sun, even at night. He would make thunder and lightning appear on a clear day. He would cause different sounds to appear in heaven. He would raise the dead on their way to be buried. At a mere thought, He would walk through walls. Without thinking, He would walk on the surface of water. He would speak, and a host of heavenly angels would appear. He would mount up against the sky on different occasions and rebuke the winds.

Today, it may seem and prove difficult for ordinary folks of the church to conceive of their Lord and Master to accomplish such feats, looking at them from their everyday humane side. But if Jesus is ruler over the Kingdom of God and is the Messiah of the world and is the Redeemer of mankind, and came to save the world, and is the creator of everything of nature, and is the light of the world, and is the Bright and Morning Star, and baptized with the Holy Ghost and with fire, whose exact lineage leads to the very Garden of Eden, and He rose up to defeat the most powerful force of nature (Luke 4:13), what more could there have been to be done by Him? Yet there is far more that was done than what was actually recorded in the realm of the four gospels during the ruling three years of His earthly and public ministry. There were miracles and signs and wonders beyond those known from the gospels, which are far too awesome to gaze upon as causing the top of heaven to tighten at the very top at His spoken command. He did not seek fame, but it went out of Him into every country.

Thinking back on the evening in which He conveyed Himself into the mountain for an all-night prayer, so many wonders leap off the pages of scriptures that it is very difficult for me to record some of them. They are so full of scriptural wonders. After His all-night prayer, He came down from the mountain with the disciples and stood on the plain of the valley floor. A great multitude of people out of all Judaea and Jerusalem and from the sea coast of the Tyre and Sidon, standing there on the floor of the plain, surrounded by His disciples and a great multitude of people, Jesus began to radiate great trains and waves of energy in such radiating quantities of virtue that the whole multitude sought to touch Him. There went virtue out of Him and healed them all. Jesus was their dynamo and a magnitude of power for multitudes.

Most of the powers possessed by Jesus have not come down to the understanding of the church (from the revelation of Matthew 28:18).

It is not only in the case of the raising of Lazarus from the dead, causing him to levitate the forty-two steps up out of his tomb up to the presence of Jesus who called him that Jesus caused others to levitate also. But first, let us clear the case of Lazarus's levitation before we further amaze you with the scripture. In John 11:44, he who was dead came forth. That is amazing enough in itself, but he was bound, hand and foot, and in grave clothes. Not only was he wrapped as a mummy but his face was also bound with a napkin. He could not walk; he could not use his hand to balance himself, and he could not see where he was going.

Under these circumstances, how could he stand before Jesus, who called him forth? Apparently, he was still bound when he arrived before Jesus when Jesus said loose him and let him go. If you cannot clearly see the dead coming forth through levitation by the command of Jesus himself, perhaps you live close enough to Jesus yourself to have him prove these papers wrong about Himself throughout the four gospels and beyond.

In the other amazing cases of Jesus causing others to levitate, if other facts can be drawn about His most amazing feats of the scriptures, at least great waves of levitation can be drawn from a great deal of biblical knowledge in anticipation of the great power that He possesses and of those great wonders that He performs.

His ministry began at the Jordan River, which separated the children of Israel from the Promised Land after Egypt. This Jordan was rich in Jewish history through Joshua, David, Elijah, and now John. Much can be obtained about the rift through extensive study. It began in the north near Mount Hermon above sea level, flows south to the sea upon which Jesus would walk, and onward to the Dead Sea, nearly a hundred miles totally. This most prominent river in the Bible would also be the ideal place to manifest wonders to all Israel by baptizing Jesus here (Matt. 3:13–17, Mark 1:9–11, Luke 3:21–23) according to John 1:31.

Upon very close examination of these three scriptural baptismal recordings at the Jordan, the beginning of the miraculous powers of Jesus would be seen to manifest themselves to begin His public ministry. Are these mighty powers that are now being revealed in their array for greatness beyond the belief of many? Yes.

Now as to other amazing cases of Jesus causing others in the scriptures to levitate in a most miraculous manner, we take you to the day that He would display miraculous feats of levitation after conveying Himself away, up onto a mountain (Mark 3:13). A simple question would be asked: How do you know where He would go if you are not there to see where He went or in what direction He went if you did not accompany Him? But clearly, He goeth up onto a mountain. Was he seen going into a cave of the mountain, rather than being seen going onto the mountain? And He calleth unto Him whom He would. That is, the choice is made by Jesus himself while in this mountain, whom He would himself call, and they came unto Him. He called whom he would, just as He called whom he did when He particularly called Lazarus, and he came unto Him.

It is as difficult for the world today, as it was difficult for the world then to behold individual levitation and human conveyance occurring all around them at the command of the Son of the Living God. Individual levitation and human conveyance occurring beyond the understanding of nonbelievers had devastating effects upon those of Jesus's day. In the case of the man with the withered hand (Luke 6:8), Jesus commanded him to rise up, that is, levitate and stand forth in that levitation in the midst, and he arose and stood forth in that levitation. This was an act that filled nonbelievers with madness (Luke 6:11).

It was in these days of His ministry that Jesus conveyed himself away more often than other days to continue in prayer all night. It was in this cycle of conveyance that great waves of virtue radiated from Him.

Now that we have established these great many impossibilities with Jesus, even beyond some of those recorded in the gospels, surpassing those wonders done earlier by those in the scripture who had less power than He himself; it is now time to look at Jesus away from the flat page and one-dimensional version of ignorance of Him. To stop imagining that fictitious and animated drawings of folklore and cartoon characters have more powers than He himself. With Him only is everything possible, and we need to see Him in that everything possibility mode and not try to only imagine that with Him all things are possible but to apply our faith in Him more forcefully until we see at least these revealed glories of Him from the pages of these four gospels.

Let's examine the time that He awoke a great while before day, and he went out (Mark 1:35). Note the extension after He awoke early before day that He went out. Surely there can be no further extension than a person arising and going out. But note further: He departed, Himself alone into a solitary place and prayed. Remember Him calling unto himself whom He would, well the group that were with Simon somehow followed after Him (Mark 3:13). As surely as Jesus departed and they followed after Him, it also means that they also departed in the very same way as a group of followers. But also take note that in verse Mark 1:38, Let us (as in let us make man) go into the next towns. Looking even closer, we are going into other towns together that I may preach in them also, but it is because of this preaching, came I forth. And how came I forth? Through conveyance, and this conveyance was throughout all Galilee.

Now let us look at the event with this beseeching leper in verse Mark 1:40. In verse 41, Jesus moved with compassion and put forth His hand. Surely Jesus was not standing upon the ground when He put forth His precious hand and touched him. Note in verse 35 that Jesus departed and how He departed. No sooner than Jesus spoke to the leper and the disease departed, likewise did the cleansed man depart forthwith, and Jesus sent Him to Jerusalem to the priest, for a testimony unto them, quite a distance south from Galilee.

There are some who may be maddened at the thought of Jesus having Simon and the others that were with him follow him, in seeing the effect of Jesus upon the group that conveyed themselves after Him. When the effect of envy and disbelief with unacceptance sat upon the Pharisees who took counsel with the Herodians to destroy Jesus (Mark 3:6), note that in verse 7, Jesus withdrew Himself with His disciples to the sea. It was awe-inspiring to see Jesus with His disciples suspended in safety out over the sea and away from destruction on shore.

You may ask, why so much of the gospel of Mark? Well, being the first completed and published gospel works of Jesus, with the epistles of the apostle Paul being the exception, which were published before these writings of Mark, it is about the nature, powers, and living accounts of the publications of His public ministry. Therefore, this beginning of the gospel of Jesus Christ, the Son of the Living God in (Mark 1:1) has its rightful place about who Jesus Christ really is through the gospel. Before the time the apostle Paul completed his epistles of his writings on Jesus, Mark had not yet completed his gospel on Jesus. It is within this period, the unwritten period, even after the end of the three years of Jesus's ministry, and although the apostles were still alive, that the greatest interest was drawn away from the greatest wonders accomplished by Jesus during His three-year ministry by the apostles themselves.

Even the twenty-six-year inquisition of those upon whom Jesus had performed miracles at Jerusalem was finished by eyewitnesses and personal accounts of Him before any published writings of His. The real truth about those true wonders of Jesus began to fade into the memories of the beholders of them.

Although the great wonders of Jesus began to fade into the memories of those before that inquisition, when the man born blind of the ninth chapter of the gospel of John, being one of the inquisitors and eyewitness of Him (John 9:37), the holy anointing that filled the whole area within the three-hundred-mile radius of His ministry, is the potent and electrifying era of wonders that inspired these Jesus papers. It was here that amazement upon amazement of wonders is performed by Jesus. It was here that He actually performed wonders, as many as God Almighty assigned upon the environment and circuit of travel.

It is assumed that the reader is aware of the differences between levitation, conveyance, and ascendance by Jesus, and that these papers of Him would also bring home the understanding of these differences about Him. These papers would again make the whole world as amazed and electrified as it was made in the more than one thousand days of His ministry then. As Jesus himself would put it in John 9:5, as long as I am in the world, I am the light of the world. Having this luminosity of mind, with affective works of authority over the world, the only remedy remaining is its proof. These proofs were assured by the manifestations of those inexhaustible powers being far too wonderful for the mere minds of synagogue worshipping. Probably the last act of temple ceremony honored by God himself in the temple at Jerusalem was the sending forth of the angel Gabriel to Zacharias about the foretelling of the birth of the forerunner in Luke 1:13. For a clearer comprehension of this last honored act within the temple itself at Jerusalem, see John 4:21, where Jesus himself drew true faith and worship away from the temple at Jerusalem. Even in this last honored act by God, in sending Gabriel, this was not fully received by a ceremonial priest blamelessly walking in all the commandments and ordinances of the Lord (Luke 1:18). There had to be a need, and this need would be fulfilled at the time of life for both John and Jesus. One shall be great in the sight of the Lord; and the other shall be called the Son of the Highest (Luke 1:15 and Luke 1:32).

Those things, which Jesus would do and actually did, were those things from the highest order and greatly surpassed the very nature and mind of those ordinary things done anywhere else in the whole world. There is, at the very start of His ministry, little wonder that such a great manifestation occurred at the Jordan. For the path of He, who is great in the sight of God, and He, who is Son of the Highest, met in the fulfillment of time and the fulfilling of all righteousness, for the manifestation before all Israel at the Jordan. These papers wish to move within that area of Jesus's ministry where wonders are fresh and staggering beyond the ignorance and disbelief that surfaced not long after those days of Pentecost when even before then, the false rumor was believed that His disciples came by night and stole Him away while we slept (Matt. 28:13). Be sure to include verse 15. The cover-up was commonly reported at the time that Matthew took a pen in hand to write his gospel.

How hypocritical it is to behold great magnitudes of wonders performed by the Son of the Living God of unequal proportions and still fear the loss of your life by those who openly manifest hatred and destruction against Him. Also see fear from the other side (John 9:22), of being put out of the synagogue because of Him. Great oppositions and fears giving cause for proper historical facts and more manifestations for wonders performed by Jesus were already at work during His tenure on earth.

Moving Jesus beyond the two fish and five loaves of bread, beyond the wine at the wedding, beyond the raising of Lazarus from the dead, and beyond just walking upon the Sea of Galilee, should not cause a great earthquake even in today's world, in view of what Jesus himself allowed in (John 14:12). The works that I do, shall ye do also. Now the question to the church is when? When will those of the church do the works that I do, as allowed by Jesus himself? Or when will the opportunities present themselves to execute (John 5:20), for even greater works than any of these to be shown?

When Jesus was presenting these things to the public through His ministry, of these great free works to be done by those who heard Him, how much fear and doubt filled the poor hearts of those poor merchants, farmers and shepherds who had in no way experienced anything near the likes of things seen that were done by Jesus himself. According to John 14:12, all it took was the matter of believing on Him for the good of things and for the doing of these works of wonders.

What great power then does belief have, especially on Him? Every living Christian should be able to answer this question in professing belief in Christ Jesus. Yet according to the New Testament, the number of people in Jesus's days that performed any wonders or likable works was the bare minimal. These works performed by them were of no great magnitude with reference to John 14:12.

The apostle John did observe someone doing menial work in Jesus's ministry days (Mark 9:38), and they forbid him of doing even this. Although this menial work was done through faith in Jesus's name, the simple belief in His name would cause the simplest works to be performed by such believers. But do not take such a seemingly simple thing to be so simple as believing in how great a power such a seemingly simple thing possesses.

There is a great amount of biblical knowledge to be obtained by the usage of His name alone, which would occupy pages among these Jesus papers other than the apostle John and others observing one casting out adversaries by it (Mark 9:38). Another example of the effect of the power of His name is spoken of by the apostle Peter in Acts 4:12. Not the power to cast out adversaries (Mark 9:38) nor the power to cure impotency (Acts 3:16) nor the power to render salvation anywhere under heaven (Acts 4:12), but by that name to render power to transform any to become the sons of God (John 1:12). Within the sphere of the works during the time of Jesus among all the mighty acts of wonders He performed in His ministry, this is the power of transformation most lacking in His own day in order to perform the exact works that He allotted in John 14:12. The performance of these allotted works, of which He did alone, did not include those greater works offered nor of those offered thereafter, which are greater still. Now what does that power of belief cause to happen in the life of the believer of Christ? No one is more qualified to give an answer to this question than Jesus himself.

In John 11:40, Jesus said that if thou wouldest believe, thou shouldest see the glory of God. Some of you are partially right when you think that Jesus speaks in the hereafter about the glory of God being revealed to the believers. Speaking to the apostles earlier in John 11:4, Jesus said, "This sickness is not unto death because he hath not given me over unto death" (Ps. 118:18). Therefore, this sickness is for the glory of God that the Son of God might be glorified thereby.

This grand knowledge is good for those who simply wish to believe in Jesus, which is good, or who wishes to believe in His name, which is also good. But firmly note John 3:16, carefully examining what is written therein in the very same way you had to very carefully examine John 3:3 on seeing the Kingdom of God in John 3:5. Now upon close examination of John 3:16, which reads that whosoever believeth in Him <u>should</u> not perish. A more dominant word of security and certainty is that whosoever believeth in Him <u>shall</u> not perish. This point of believing on Him or believing in Him could be further revealing from John 8:31. There, Jesus said to those Jews, which believed on Him, take note that these are those, which believed on Him and who ought to see the glory of God, or they ought not to perish. To the amazement of the reader of these believers in John 8:59: Then they took up stones to cast at Him. But Jesus vanished into a shadow, went out of the temple, going on through the midst of them. Very similar to those crying Hosanna, who afterward cried, crucify Him.

With so much against Jesus in His day with His ministry, the Pharisees and lawyers (Luke 7:30), the elders and the chief priests and scribes (Luke 9:22), the betrayers, and lack of faith in the disciples, it is little wonder that the pure knowledge of His great magnitude of wonders and miracles have yet to reach the church today. The involvement of skills, the working of principles, the combination of fields of study and learning has advanced progress within the world and has sent forth the world with its workings ahead of the church. These workings have covered over those mighty wonders of Christ Jesus, which ought to be done in accordance with His allowance. Are we saying that engineering on all fronts, aviation, and engineering of the sciences, the designing and building of satellites and pay loaders, refineries for chemicals, gigantic earthmovers of power dams and ore mining should not come into their own? No, not at all. For it is these great fields of knowledge, along with other fields of communication that have caused society and the world to advance in automation and telecommunications while those who are sent forth to preach have to sometimes wonder, to whom do we preach in such an advanced world as this?

It is a sad thing when death takes away world attention from itself in mass destruction of its inhabitants, but earthquakes, flash floods, twisters, and famines had to be used to regain the world's attention when it goes out of control and away from standing guidelines of sovereignty. But let us not forget that Jesus testified against it in His time about the men thereof (John 3:19) because their deeds were evil and against the very works thereof (John 7:7) that the works thereof of them are evil. Jesus has proven that they will not survive. Jesus has proven that they would not have gotten any better (Luke 17:22). Other than the works thereof being evil, the days will come when ye shall desire, because of evil, to see one of the days of the Son of Man. Evil deeds and evil works in a world of evil people, according to Matthew 7:11 and Luke 11:13 amongst holy people will bring about the desire of those days of the Son of Man. For the thoughts for the world each day forward, take thought for the things of itself. And this evil for the day is sufficient unto the day.

What is one of the days of the Son of Man of which the world would desire to see? In Luke 13:32, Jesus said, "Behold, I cast out adversaries, and I do cures today and tomorrow, and the third day I shall be perfected." Needless to say, the world ought to desire His cures today and tomorrow.

We have lingered in the ordinary long enough in these papers about the extraordinary and marvelous wonders of Jesus beyond the interception of the world's view about Him.

THE TRUTHFUL REALIZATION OF JESUS

THE FRAILTIES OF DOUBT and disbelief and the fear of reprisal, not to mention ignorance and other environmental traffic, has put some of the greatest exploits of Jesus away from the view of history and treasured memories and moments of Him.

The truthful realization of Jesus over the world's ignorance of Him, and of the unbelievable attainment of His powers would channel the whole world and its system onto another, and an unheard of course, never before thought to exist within the course of the history of man.

In Mark 3:13, He conveyed himself onto a mountain. Now to you who find it hard for God, with whom all things are possible, to convey himself away at will should consider the reason behind the three days for Jesus himself having to walk, confined to merely just walking a memorial for prophets not to perish (Luke 13:33). What then will be His mode of transportation after His third-day walk memorial?

The ordinary way of seeing Jesus is in the customary and humane way on the grounded level, in keeping Jesus within grounded based issues. Jesus would say in Mark 2:5, "Son, thy sins be forgiven thee, and the world, just as here with the scribes sitting here, began reasoning against His power." Therefore, Jesus must now resort to a higher than ground issue. In Mark 2:10, He reveals that He would remarkably display that power to speak to cause to levitate. In Mark 2:12, they exclaimed, "We never saw it in this fashion. There has never been a man in Capernaum in this fashion along the northwestern shore of the Galilee. Note that the man sick of the palsy arose immediately, took up his bed, and went forth. He went straight forth before them all in such a way that they were all amazed, and glorified God. And note also in Mark 2:13, He also went forth again by the seaside, and all the multitude resorted after Him. Would you dare to behold the shadow of a resorting multitude by the seaside?

The multitude of Capernaum resorted after Him, caught up to him, and He taught them, having seen that God gives such power to men (Matt. 9:8). Jesus himself had already proven that He had power Himself (Matt. 9:6), but the multitudes marveled and glorified God, which had given such power unto men. And the sky-streaking question is: Men, where is your power today given to you by God? At least in the days of God with Jesus?

Having taught the multitudes a worthy lesson of heavenly things, He was off again to appoint Levi, retiring him from the receipt of custom to prepare him to write the first placed gospel of His New Testament. Jesus did not pass from these resorted multitudes by foot, as He passed by the son of Alphaeus.

The variations shown of the exact incidents and events of Jesus being parallel among the gospels are of no use to these papers of Jesus. That has been given over to other writers for those less fortunate. But as of the Jesus papers, the bridegroom is with them. Amen.

When He taught the resorting multitudes heavenly things, unlike seeing the multitudes when he conveyed Himself and went up into the mountain drawing, the then appointed apostles after Himself, indeed preludes to being caught up (1 Thess. 4:17), this lesson on heavenly things was unlike the Sermon on the Mount (Matt. 5:1–7, 27).

THE BRILLIANT TEACHINGS OF JESUS

IN A GREAT MANY cases, the ignorance of the people brought out some of the best teachings of Jesus. These papers will only highlight a few of them,

Let us look at the case of the scribes and Pharisees sitting in the home of Jesus at Capernaum (Mark 2:16) and entered into the house of Jesus there, with opposition to His own houseguests. They say unto the disciples, how is it that He eateth and drinketh with publicans and sinners? Jesus is found to always be true to His teachings and to His instructions. In Luke 14:12, He taught that when thou makest a dinner or a supper, call not thy friends nor thy brethren. But when thou makest a feast (Luke 14:13), call the poor, the maimed, the lame, and the blind. In other words, call the sick (Mark 2:17). The calling of sinners to repentance point to: Thou shalt be recompensed at the resurrection of the just (Luke 14:14).

Now speaking of their custom of the fasting of the disciples of John and of the Pharisees, hey come and say to Him; why do the disciples of John and of the Pharisees fast, but thy disciples fast not? (Mark 21:18, Matt. 9:14, and Luke 5:33). The lesson from these illustrious parables is that the new is for the new.

We will now turn to a firsthand authentic writing and an eyewitness account of the power in operation of those wonders which Jesus himself did as were recorded by Levi, the son of Alphaeus, and by John, the son of Zebeede. These papers will not change their observations of those wonders of Christ recorded by either apostle, Matthew or John, who both actually gave eyewitness accounts of those things about Jesus in the flesh.

After His miraculous manifestation, which is actually recorded by Matthew, who was not yet a disciple of Jesus, Matthew was called away from the receipt of custom. John, on the other hand, was called away from his father's boat after that manifestation. The apostle John did speak of this manifestation of Jesus through John the Baptist (John 1:31). Both Matthew and the apostle John may have gotten this manifestation from the very lips of John the Baptist, who was a catalyst in this monumental manifestation that began the ministry of Jesus to the world.

Previous knowledge has gone forward in these papers to inform the readers what to expect from the pages of these two gospels, and Jesus's powers in these miracles will not lessen. It is very easy to say that Jesus performed thirty-three miracles, which may have been witnessed by Levi and John. Upon closer examinations of their recordings of them, even they themselves agree upon their limitations in recording them.

Both writers began their record in antiquity. Matthew began in human antiquity while John began his in etymology. These beginnings are not to throw the readers of the gospels off but to cultivate and to prepare them for the importance of Jesus through recorded history.

Beginning with antiquity, lineage is important to history to reveal the presence of God working on both human and human speech fronts. Both move their records right up to the time of Jesus to begin His public ministry (Matt. 3:13 and John 1:29). We will be led up of the Spirit of God in these papers of Jesus and will resort to other gospels as the Spirit seeks further proof of them. We will analyze the gospel of John basically because Jesus has promised Nathanael, meaning the giver of God (John 1:50): Thou shalt see greater things than these. The magnitude of this great promise of the truths of these greater things would only be dwarfed by those doing greater works than themselves.

The Cana incident manifested forth in the water changing. We have seen the effects of those who believe in His name. We have cleared up the Judge Nicodemus error and corrections.

The teachings, the sayings, the parables, the words, the miracles, the signs, and the wonders of Jesus are more than what is recorded within the four gospels, even including those recorded as eyewitness accounts of Him by Matthew, John, and Peter himself, who was a constant companion with John more than anyone else with the exception of James, the brother of John.

The ignorance of Judge Nicodemus prompted the knowledge of earthly things, much like the ignorance of the world in olden days prompted the revelations of priestly arts, which were hidden away from the ordinary through the revealed works of Moses when he revealed them through his acts before the king of Egypt. Suppose Judge Nicodemus had not stolen away to Jesus by night. Would man still have known that he must be born again? Yes. Would this earthly necessity for the renewal of man have been known by means other than by Judge Nicodemus? Yes. And how do we know this? We know this by the later experience taking place on the road to Damascus. For it was said of necessity in Acts 9:15: Go thy way: For he is a chosen vessel unto me, to bear my name before the Gentiles and kings and the children of Israel. Just as John the Baptist was sent that Jesus should be made manifest to Israel (John 1:31), had Judge Nicodemus not stolen away to see Jesus by night or had the apostle Paul not been on his way to persecute the church, you can rest assured that these solutions to these necessities would have been met, even if John the Baptist himself had not been used as the forerunner for Jesus's manifestation to Israel. Simply because the time was full for these things to occur in the course of history, conversions, and adjustments had to be made to comply with the times for their fulfillment. Scripture cannot be broken (John 10:35) and all this was done so that the scriptures of the prophets might be fulfilled (Matt. 26:56).

This could not have been a case of necessity with Jesus himself, for He did come as God the Creator of all things, who also govern all things in heaven and on earth. He said: If any man shall say to you, lo, here is Christ; or lo, He is there; believe him not (Mark 13:21). He came of His own necessity in the fullness of His own time to do as He himself decreed, as it pleased himself according to His own Holy Counsel and Godhead. He could have created and used another Paul; He could have created and used another Judge Nicodemus, but there was no room for substance to create and use another Jesus. For He himself is the only self-created God, having the power beforehand to create of necessity that and those things, which pleased him. Whether they be in heaven or on earth, whether they be myself or you or He. Men look at the atoms, which God created. They also look at atomic actions and other creations of God from the beginning of the creation, which God created from the beginning unto this time. They see them and their atomic patterns as great building blocks of nature and for the whole universe and cosmos, their structures, their patterns, and their atomic collections and transfers account for whatever patterns that presently stand finished and comprising everything there from themselves. When trees put forth their leaves, we know that summer is near.

Because of the ignorance of Judge Nicodemus of earthly necessities, the world discovers that man must be born again, and because of the world discovering that man must be born again, the revelation points to that by which man is to be born again. From that revelation pointing toward the Kingdom of God, that by which man is to enter there into is revealed (John 3:5). Now since we are into these papers at great biblical depths and that cannot be biblically denied, and since we marvel not that Jesus saith unto us, we must be born again of water and of the Spirit in order to enter the Kingdom of God (John 3:5). We read in Luke 17:21: Behold, the Kingdom of God is within you. The question may be asked, how do you enter into that Kingdom of God that is within us? It is revealed in Luke 17:20 that the Kingdom of God cometh not with observation, and this is the truth since there is no one within you but you yourself. Therefore, no one else can possibly observe the Kingdom of God that is within you unless they can observe that kingdom, given in the way that Jesus said that it ought to be observed in Matthew 5:16. Let your light so shine before men that they may see your good works, and glorify your Father, which is in heaven. But how do you get there from within yourself? Well, according to John 3:5, except a man be born of water and of the Spirit, he cannot enter into the Kingdom of God, which did not come with observation. But also, according to Luke 18:17, whosoever shall not receive the Kingdom of God as a little child, shall in no way enter therein either. Why is it hard for a rich man to enter into the Kingdom of God (Luke 18:25)?

Therefore, in order to enter into that kingdom according to John 3:5, a man must be born of water and of the Spirit first or else he cannot enter into the Kingdom of God. Then he must receive the Kingdom of God as a little child, or shall in no way enter there (Luke 18:17). See Matthew 18:3 for the apostles to enter into the Kingdom of Heaven, and see Matthew 11:11, for nevertheless, he that is least in the Kingdom of Heaven is greater than John. There is very much knowledge about the Kingdom of God throughout the New Testament and gospel.

Jesus also takes the occasion to further inform Judge Nicodemus about the principle and law of ascendance, which is a thing of knowledge from Heaven. In John 3:13, He lays down the format: No man hath ascended up to Heaven but He that came down from Heaven. Here is that law of ascendance. If you did not come down, you cannot return, and who should know better than Him who made all things. His word is law.

Judge Nicodemus prided himself, sitting high on the Sanhedrin Council as a master of the law, as a highly cultured mind. But Jesus takes occasion to cultivate other facts of importance to the world by using the available mind of one so cultivated to introduce other important facets and truths that are important to the whole world. The same opportunity occurred for John 3:16. Some say this meeting place in Jerusalem belonged to the apostle John, but you judge, which is more important, the place where they meet or the ideas imparted here by Jesus, the Son of God?

Other illustrious ideas that Jesus imparted were, this is the condemnation (John 3:19) and he that doeth truth (John 3:21). These teachings and revelations are far from signs and wonders done by Jesus, but the opportunity is afforded for teaching them.

Now Jesus and the disciples came into the land of Judaea, but it is not recorded that they all were conveyed or transported there from Jerusalem. We do know that He tarried there with them for a while in their baptismal work of the kingdom, south of where John the Baptist was also baptizing. The apostles came northward to John and were also baptized by him. For if it seemed right for John to baptize Jesus, it would also seem right for the apostles to have John baptize them also. They came and were baptized. The revelation of the profound truth and way with God is given by John the Baptist in John 3:34. He whom God hath sent speaketh the words of God. Is this not the way with God? That confirmeth the work of His servant and performeth the counsel of His messengers (Isa. 44:26). (See John 8:26, John 8:47, and John 8:42). God does not measure the spirit of the ones He sends into the world.

There can be no doubt as to that mode of transport, which Jesus employed when He left Judaea and departed again into Galilee farther to the north. But He must be transported through Sychar of Samaria. The need for this venture will be made manifest, as was the need revealed by Jesus of the revelation of the widower with Elijah to the Jews about Zarephath, as the two names opposes one another. (Sychar meaning falsehood and Zarephath meaning refining.)

Some may say if Jesus left Judaea and departed into Galilee again, (John 4:3), and that He must needs go through Samaria (John 4:4), being wearied with His journey (John 4:6), and sat thus on the well at the sixth hour (which is according to the reckoning of time, twelve noon, before the encounter with the woman. While sitting on the well as recorded in John 4:6, please note that finally after departing again repeatedly into Galilee, which is north of Sychar at this date and time, He needed go through Samaria, which is also north of Sychar, but is also southwest of Galilee. Even in Salem is where John baptized the apostles, its location is northeast of the village Sychar, on the main road from Jerusalem to the south, and Galilee to the north. If you truly knew Jesus and how He labored from day to day within His three-year ministries of healing, making the lame walk, keeping with the law that He fulfills, casting out unclean spirits, teaching, commanding, and a great number of other things, you would understand being wearied with His journey.

Here another opportunity presents itself for clarification in the most magnificent way. For the place of falsehood (Sychar) is about to have some of the most profound truths revealed within her that still lay hidden away from most of today's societies and the church.

There is a deep communication between Jesus and this Samaritan woman at noon at the well. Most will know of this communication at this well, but deeper and greater things with purpose are to arrive from this unusual meeting at the well of Samaria in Sychar. Falsehood is about to be made real by the truth. Now why would God, in the person of Jesus, ask a woman to give Him water without some purpose behind it? What is to be discerned from this meeting and communication at Sychar? What can we draw out now and bear unto you, who hears?

The purpose behind the request to give me water to drink (John 4:7) is to reveal a revelation beyond the salvation of the true and newly identified purpose of God and the new and true mode of worshipping Him other than at Jerusalem by the Jewish people. This will become very clear as we go on without signs and wonders being done by Jesus here. The opportunity now is for these new, other than Jewish, revelations. The very same things Jesus taught about the prophet Elijah being sent to the widower at Zarephath, or Sarepta (Luke 4:25–26). But unto none of them was Jesus sent, save unto Sychar, a village of Samaria, unto a woman that is a widower. Is it not best to allow Jesus to identify himself within scripture, especially when He himself is speaking them out of His own mouth?

It depends on the depth and perception of the human mind that determines what and how you believe (John 3:18). By having the only begotten depth, the only begotten perception, and the only begotten mind, can you identify the true nature of salvation as His believers? If your mind is not of falsehood (Sychar), and you have understood these things with peace and contentment, you will no longer be led astray of the truth of the gospel about the works of Jesus, nor of those powers He possesses away from the way that the earth portrays Him using them.

Here we are at Sychar by an earthly well with a woman who knew not the gift of God (Rom. 6:23), which is eternal life, nor who it is that saith to her, give me water to drink. You had to have known what you asked for in order to know what you were expected to receive. She did not know anything about the giving of living water nor did she know anything about the gift of God being eternal life. But what she did know was traditional history.

It is indeed a strange question to ask the creator of all mankind if He himself is less than any of His creatures. She held onto traditional history, even in worship. But neither in this mountain, nor yet at Jerusalem shall they worship the Father. It is here that Jesus reveals through Isaiah 28:5 the true worshippers and our present mode of worship, in spirit and in truth.

The very hour has come for the true worshippers to emerge in Sychar, a name meaning falsehood. But take note how before this event, history has shown man seeking the Lord to worship Him (Deut. 4:29 and Isa. 55:6). But that was the introduction of this event or the revelation of the true worshippers. It is now the Father, who seeks such to worship Him. Where has the Father found you? And He will only find you if you are a true worshipper of Him. The opportunity has arrived here for Jesus to make known what kind of spirit that God is and that worship of Him in spirit and in truth is required.

I do not fault the writers of the gospels. I thank God for them, giving us the life of Jesus, even in those portions written about Him in scripture. But even though they were inspired, they still seem to be governed in their writings by the ignorance of the people of their day. Instead of focusing more on the dynamic power of Jesus with amazement and thrilling delight, they found it easier to record a few borderline miracles and wonders of healing and casting out a few unclean spirits. These things are true about Him, but there is so much more in truth about Him also.

Do bear with me for just a little while and allow me to remove the veil of ignorance and deception that has been cast over the whole world and under which it labors. How did the wicked deceiver take Jesus up into an exceedingly high mountain? (Matt. 4:8) Or how did he take Jesus up into the Holy City and set Him on a pinnacle of the temple? (Matt. 4:5) Was it not that because he had the power to convey also? Do not be frightened because the wicked deceiver has the power to convey. Those powers and dynamics, which are manifested by Jesus in comparison to his power, is a grain of sand in the universe.

It is good that the writers of the gospels gave much about the teachings of Jesus and of what He thought and believed in, being God himself. It is also good that they wrote down things that He said, though many of them understood not. It is also good to see Jesus's long-range vision and authority and beholding His long-range consignments and establishments. It is good to hear Jesus say the works that I do bear witness of me, that the Father hath sent me.

Jesus said on one occasion, "No man can come to me except the Father, which hath sent me, draw Him." (John 6:44) Now some of you may ask, how can I equate these kinds of power dynamics of Christ with the world of the philosophers? Truthfully, you cannot equate them at all because He made all things, but the fulfillment of time came after the philosophers.

We read that Jesus went over the Sea of Galilee (John 6:1). It is easy to see Him conveyed over the sea. Jesus went over the Sea of Galilee (John 6:1), and a great multitude followed Him. Now how did the great multitude follow Him, being under the attraction of His great power? Was it not also over the Sea of Galilee, which is the Sea of Tiberias?

We know of leading stars of the heavens, leading massive star fields both across and around the heavens in timeless succession. Such actions are charted for thousands of years for different but massive star fields, which weigh in tons compared to a single star weight in comparison to a greater multitude, which is almost zero, or you may argue that its weightlessness is due to cosmic distance. Well, at some cosmic distances, the density of some stars are so compressed that only a few particles of mass would supersede the whole weight of the mass of the great multitude, and do not forget John 1:3, and that includes everything.

The miracles that Jesus did on those that were diseased are enough to fill more volumes about Him. But we find Him transporting himself again up onto a mountain.

Come near ye nations to hear, and hearken ye people. Let the earth hear and all that is therein, the world and all things that come forth of it. The very truth of Jesus through these papers taken from the gospels can at last be told. Jesus went up onto a mountain with His disciples and there He sat with them.

The translation of one substance into another substance is not the same as the multiplication of any one substance or of the multiplication of any other one substance. Molecular transformation is a proven theory and an act of nature wherein one molecular substance ends in the transformation process and the other molecular substance began from the same molecular transformation process. Equations identifying their molecular configurations are prominent. You may also wish to consider the nuclear fusion process to satisfy the inquisitive mind. But Jesus's multiplication of five barley loaves and two small fish (John 6:9) was not from the geometry of a flat and one-dimensional entity resulting in mathematical theory. Through the geometries, all sections of the sphere are a cone and known, but nothing biological has ever risen from the geometries. But with Jesus, fish and bread, though multiplied by His power and scripture, are gone through the multiplication in their same nature and substance. The power to take multiplication through its primary nature and substance without the lack of theory seems possessed only by Jesus alone. The fish remain fish, even when cooked, and the loaves remain loaves, even when baked.

Jesus always withdrew Himself at will with His disciples to the sea. But on the occasion that they came and took Him by force to make Him a king (John 6:15), He departed again onto a mountain, himself alone. This sense of travel is only ignorant to those blinded by their intelligence of the world order. In the days of the sons of the prophets, it was not an astounding thing to suggest, lest peradventure, the spirit of the Lord hath taken Him up and cast Him upon some mountain or into some valley (2 Kings 2:16). It is easy for them to behold the spirit of the Lord at work in such transports, even in their day long ago. After departing himself to the mountain to escape being made king, the disciples went down to the sea, entered into a ship, and went over the sea toward Capernaum. It was now dark, so those familiar with the wind tunnel of the Galilee will understand its rising by reason of a great wind on this particular night. Out across the turbulent sea and through the darkness, opposite from the direction of the shore, they see the outline of an approaching figure drawing nigh unto the ship, and they were afraid. But the figure said unto them on the water, "It is I; be not afraid."

That same figure that transported itself again onto a mountain earlier and remained there until darkness was not walking upon the sea in defiance of the laws of buoyancy and gravity, and was about to defy the laws of aerodynamics because when he entered the ship on this occasion, immediately the ship was at the land whither they went.

He overtook both the forces of labor and sail. What a Savior! If you desire to walk on water like Peter did, other forms of defiance of nature is required.

A very clear as crystal understanding is in need for these particular teachings and standards of Jesus, as He differentiates between the world standards and those standards of Heaven, the example of manner being given by Moses to the children of Israel only (John 6:32) and the true bread from Heaven given unto the world (John 6:33). Only those who were associated with Moses in their wanderings were allowed to eat manna. But the Bread of God is He, which cometh down from Heaven. Note the difference between this bread, which the Lord hath given you to eat (Exod. 16:15) for those of Israel and the Bread of God, who is He, who cometh down from Heaven and giveth life unto the world (John 6:33). See the standards set also for the extreme differences between water (John 4:13–14) and worship (John 4:21–24).

JESUS

NO ONE IN TODAY'S society has had the chance to really focus on Jesus. Not really. If what has come down through history about Him was intended to cause the world excitement, it is apparent that the world was not moved by his arrival or the Father's business that he came to do. But He, who healed all manner of sickness and all manner of diseases; He, who cast out unclean spirits and brought the dead back to life; He, who bore all the sickness and sins of all mankind in His own body; He, who conveyed himself away into mountains and across seas, who walked upon waters, who vanished and reappeared, who transported masses into mountains and over seas, who opened the eyes of the blind and made the lame walk, who moved ships across waters at will, who gave these same powers to men; He, who died and resurrected himself; He, who descended into hell to lead those captured free; He, who ascended into Heaven and sent back power from Heaven and much, much more, is one and the same Jesus. The Jesus who turned water into wine is also the same Jesus that multiplied the fish and loaves. He is the same Jesus who saved, sanctified, and filled you up with the Holy Ghost and fire, and there are many other horizons that stagger this lowly mind in attempting to comprehend them in these papers.

You may want to compare Jesus's definition of meat and harvest (John 4:34–35) to the world's definition. As we can plainly see, the standards of Jesus are not those of the world. Consider also the man who lay by the pool before Jesus was born (John 5:5), waiting to be healed by that method, and an opportunity that he himself would never employ. He was not healed by his thirty-eight-year method at all, but by these twenty-three characters of the alphabet forming the speech of Jesus. Rise, take up thy bed, and walk. You may also wish to consider the standard for labor, which Jesus employs (John 6:27). If you wish to be engulfed within the true standardization of Jesus, then accept John 6:35, wherein, ye shall never hunger, and whereat ye shall never thirst. There are unlimited amounts of such blessings.

WAVE INTERFERENCE

WAVE INTERFERENCE CAN BE useful or not profitable under useful circumstances. It is a field of communication that is most useful in the social orders of today and is often deployed by satellites and other communications links. Why is this form of communication within these papers? Because in John 6:44, Jesus revealed that, "No man can come unto me except the Father, which hath sent me, draw him." Now you may not see electrical wiring running from you to Jesus, or from you to the Father, or from Jesus to the Father, or you may not see an electrical wiring system running between the three of you. You may not be connected to electrical transistors receiving minute electronic and micro-impulses, but whatever way the Father uses to identify those that He is to draw to Jesus, assuredly there is never a communication failure, nor is there an interruption or interference of waves, however minute or powerful. Thus, this profound system of Fatherly communication on the behalf of the Son that involves you directly, should be given more study, if by none other than yourself who is drawn by the Father himself. Between you, the Father, and Jesus himself, there is a communication link that is undoubtedly not of this world. There are many such systems of communication introduced by Jesus within the gospels.

THE WORKS OF JESUS

AS WE HAVE SAID before and we say again, the teachings of Jesus are almost unbearable for this frail-minded Son of God. And thanks be to God, it is the spirit that quickeneth; the flesh profiteth nothing (John 6:63). It is here! Here in the spirit that they shall be all taught of God (John 6:45) and without assumption. The words that I speak unto you, they are spirit, and they are life (John 6:63). For those of you who wish to pursue your system of communication revealed earlier (John 6:44) between you, Jesus, and the Father may study when it was given you in (John 6:65). For you may find that it were given unto you of my Father before the creation of the world.

Take note now of John 7:1, of how Jesus walked in Galilee, indicating that He did not always walk while transporting himself. Also take note of how His brethren address His mode of transport in John 7:3. Depart hence, and go into Judaea. To His brethren, the perfect opportunity had arrived to show these things to the world, but again Jesus introduces another one of His standards; My time is not yet come (John 7:6). Those bright students of the law around the city of Jerusalem are always well-known among the populace of the yeshiva and in the marketplace. Lest we forget, Jesus was not educated at any institution of learning there nor at the Hillel at Jerusalem. Not having been educated in their centers of learning, how many would dare think that some eighteen years earlier, before He was Bar Mitzvahed, that this deity would again appear in the temple. They would exclaim, how knowest this man letters, having never learned (John 7:15). Scripture saith, and they shall be all taught of God (John 6:45). And shall God not teach His own, godly ways and His own Son, godly works?

The doctrine of Jesus according to its use is the doctrine of everlasting life, when in use of itself. It is good to comprehend some teaching from Jesus when opportunities present themselves to the world through the gospels and the present opportunity is such an occasion at this feast of tabernacle.

You may find the execution of the doctrine of Jesus in John 6:40 and the working faith of that doctrine in John 6:47. Of course, the only obtainable knowledge of His doctrine is executed in John 7:17, the one work, which Jesus did that caused them to marvel (John 7:15) was not having the knowledge of letters, nor was it by Him teaching in their temple (John 7:14) and not being allowed within such a sacred place, having never learned among themselves or at their schools. Take firm note of John 7:14: Jesus went up into the temple and taught. When Jesus goes up, who is there to stop Him? (You may refer back to Matt. 4:5 and 8). Of those cases, He was taken up, but when Jesus goes up, there is none to stop Him, and the dynamics of the lift-to-weight ratio is not an issue with Jesus as it is with man.

Now for those who observe John 7:23 as the one work that caused the Jews to marvel (John 7:15), be aware that now, in the midst of the feast, Jesus went up. The incident of healing a man and making him every whit whole (John 7:23), which is on the Sabbath day, therefore, the time of the midst of the feast and the time of the Sabbath day.

To know Him and to know where He is from means nothing, except you also know Him who sent Jesus, who is true.

For those of you who wish to see further into this October Feast of Tabernacle, you should take into consideration that the feast began on Wednesday. Since Jesus went up in the temple in the midst of the feast, which had to be on the Sabbath day, take note of the speaking of Jesus. Are you angry at me? I have already done one work, and ye all marvel. Two totally different human expressions; in the midst of the feast, they marveled, and on the Sabbath day, they angered or take the point of view of Jesus himself. Jesus went up into the temple in the midst of the feast and said, "I have done one work, and ye all marvel. And are ye angry at me because I have made a man every whit whole on the Sabbath Day?" Verily, the crowd is as Jesus described them and both could have occurred on the Sabbath day.

On the last day, that great day of the feast, Jesus stood and cried and proclaimed, "He that believeth in me, as the scripture has said, out of his belly shall flow rivers of living water. But you must first thirst, and come unto Him to drink." Do not forget His desire to give thee living water (John 4:10). But how do you put rivers of living water into your belly, and which are the best tributaries for the belly? Since the belly cast out into the draught (Matt. 15:17), out of his belly shall not go draught, but rivers of the spirit of living water. Believe Him to receive them. It is believing Him as the scripture hath said. These rivers will never form nor ever come into existence with this doubtfulness. Lord, who hath believed our report? And to whom is the arm of the Lord revealed? (Isa. 53:1). You should request the flow of rivers of living waters springing up into everlasting life from your own belly. Amen. Do not forget the words that I speak unto you; they are spirit, and they are life (John 6:63). Therefore, believe; be quickened and start the rivers of living waters flowing. For why should you be on the brink and edge of rivers when you can be personally responsible for them? These papers would love to move forward on every front with Jesus in His ministry and will, should He provide me the spirit and the substance. It seems that the world nor the church is aware of the purpose or reason behind Jesus's choice in John 6:70. "Have not I chosen you twelve, and one of you is an adversary?" Now the questions are, why would Jesus subject His ministry to an adversary or why should He subject

His ministry to vanity? The quickest answer is in Matthew 16:18; the gates of hell shall not prevail against it. But the more lengthy answer is found in Romans 8:20; for the creature was made subject to vanity, not willingly, but by reason of Him, who hath subjected the same in hope. Therefore, as God made this whole creation and universe, and it was made subject to vanity, so also would Jesus subject His own ministry to vanity by choosing an adversary. As vanity will not stop the demise of the universe, likewise, an adversary will not stop the victory of His ministry. The church will not stop the demise of the adversary, nor He the victory of His ministry. Hell has been made for him already.

In chapter eight of the book of John after Jesus returned from the Mount of Olives, usually from prayer among other reasons, it seemed the appropriate scriptures to stoop and write on such an occasion would have been Isaiah 4:10–11 and Isaiah 54:17. We know, unlike the judge of the third chapter, that what he wrote had to come from the Old Testament law about their error of bringing only the woman to be stoned. Naturally, as they attempted to accuse her according to Moses in the law in condemning her to be stoned as was commanded, they themselves are also found guilty of sin by not keeping the whole law, of which they are attempting to accuse her of.

We have already discussed at length the meaning of Jesus being the light of that world and not the light of this world (John 17:14). Neither He nor we are from here.

Since we are discussing the light of the world, what better time to cast light on the beginning of the creation of the world, to behold the very earliest works of Jesus, which could ever be known unto man about the earliest works of the Savior.

In the beginning, when God created the heavens, mighty works of both Father and Son were in operation. The Father had some souls within the grasp of His hand while He was laying the foundation of the heavens. But the works of the Son while creation was in formation, even though it slew Him, was a work of salvation at the beginning of the creation, which no other moment can match, except when saints on judgment day are caught up in glory. Two of the most auspicious moments in the history of the world were creation and destruction, where no moment in the history of Jesus at the beginning of the creation of the universe was more defined than seeing Him protect untold numbers of saints and sons from annihilation in the cataclysm and upheaval of the creation of the universe. Thus, He was slain from the foundation of the world (Rev. 13:8). Out of the world, I have chosen you (John 15:19). We have already said that it was difficult for men to understand Jesus before, during, and afterward.

There is very much teaching of Jesus in John's gospel in which John stresses more than the wonders of Jesus. We will observe some of these remote and profound teachings of Jesus, as well as introduce other powers in association with Him. Those other powers, which are in association with Him, will meet the same criteria and standards as other principles and generalizations disassociated with the present world standard. I am the light of the world (John 8:12), but I am not of this world (John 8:23).

The words of Jesus also offer us opportunities to prove Him to ourselves. How are these opportunities proven to us by Him? When shall ye know that I do nothing of myself, when ye have lifted up the Son of Man in evidence, then shall ye know that I am He (John 8:28). How does the word of truth make you free? You cannot know truth without first knowing the spirit of truth. And hereby know we the spirit of truth; He that knoweth God heareth us, because we are of God and hereby know we, the Spirit of God. Every spirit that confesses that Jesus Christ has come in the flesh is of God. Because the spirit is truth and everyone that is of the truth heareth my voice, and my words are spirit, and they are life. Thus, by my words, you are made free. Hearing, therefore, not only the words of the holy prophets, or of the holy apostles, but moreover, hearing the living words of the living God makes you free from all of the deceptions and vanities of life because they are sanctified in freedom through truth (John 17:17).

One of the greatest revelations that bring on one accord the whole purpose of the reason for Jesus being given to the world is found of Him in this revelation. The servant abideth not in the house forever (John 14:2), but the Son abideth ever (John 8:35). In this, Jesus has revealed His all-wise primary purpose to the world.

The most complex teachings of Jesus are too complex for even the anointed minds of those of His apostles. Therefore, what of the unanointed minds of those less fortunate in the knowledge of these things about Christ Jesus? Look at the example of John 8:44 where Jesus says to those Jews, which believed in Him (John 8:31), ye are of your father the adversary. And in John 8:56, He identifies; your father Abraham. Now is your father the adversary and your father Abraham addressed as one and the same father? If then, they are addressed as one and the same father, you must agree with these papers that Jesus not only identifies Abraham as the adversary (John 8:44) but he actually calls him Abraham by name (John 8:56). It may prove difficult for those of you who are unskilled in the word to comprehend Jesus identifying Abraham as the adversary, but intense study from John 8:33 shall prove this truth of scripture to be as truthful as John 3:31. For those of you who also find it difficult to believe in these papers, in identifying Jesus's mode of transport by conveying himself away, simply read John 5:13. After Jesus had healed the man lying beside the pool before He was born, Jesus conveyed himself away, a multitude being in that place. If you are familiar with the human spirit under the circumstances of sickness with the expectation of being healed, whether by medicine or miracle, you then know that this constitutes mobs and multitudes. Therefore, compelled to escape this multitude being in that place, Jesus had to convey himself away, as he was escaping those who would have made him king (John 6:15). In John 6:38, Jesus declared, for I came down from Heaven, and that is with all heavenly powers (Matt. 28:18).

For those of you who think that there is no difference between His actual ways, let them read Isaiah 55:9. For as the heavens are higher than the earth, so are my ways higher than your ways and my thoughts than your thoughts.

This knowledge is so difficult in excellence and so overwhelming that it is nearly impossible to record these papers of Jesus. Jesus met Abraham when as the heavenly reflection of Jesus, Melchizedek served Abraham communion (Gen. 14:18), and lest ye forget, (Matt. 16:23) where Jesus called the apostle Peter an adversary also. I am using scripture to prove my points. Are you not using scripture to prove your points? These papers would rather maintain scriptural proofs to clarify scriptural truths.

There is very much about scripture and the word of God as well as powers associated with them that have not come into the knowledge of the church. Therefore, the word cannot be preached nor given to the saints. Some just don't know, and some come as a fault within pastors because of their vanity and pride.

In chapter nine of the gospel of John, as Jesus passed by, these papers do not see Jesus in any other light or mode of transport other than levitation aboveground. Lo! The works of God should be made manifest. The manifestations of the works of God like none ever manifested before are about to be revealed unto the whole world through Jesus, the Son of the Living God.

Jesus knows within himself that: I do nothing of myself (John 8:28); he also knows that: I do always those things that please Him (John 8:29), and that I can, of mine own self, do nothing (John 5:30). Jesus knows that He will show Him greater works than these, that ye may marvel (John 5:20), that this is the work of God, that ye believe on Him whom He hath sent (John 6:29), and that this is not the same as the manifestation of the works of God to glorify the Son for the glory of God. How closely did John monitor the performance of this miracle by Jesus, seeing Him in the strength of the light of the world performing the same miracle? How much did John himself comprehend of this revelation of the Father revealed by Jesus? Ye have neither heard His voice at any time nor seen His shape (John 5:37), although he knew the voice of the Father from Matthew 17:5 and had heard rumor about the voice of the Father some forty days before Jesus called him (Matt. 3:17, Matt. 4:2, and Matt. 4:21). But the comprehension of the shape of the Father was nowhere near the understanding of the apostolic mind of the revelator. Neither is it near the mind of the average church leader even today. Simply because the universe is of the shape of an ellipse surrounded by a halo is no reason for anyone to think that the shape of the Father is also elliptical. Of course, to hear His voice and to see His shape is reserved for the Son only or to those whom the Son will reveal these things to. In Him, we live, we move, and we have our being. Even if you can observe a series of such elliptical universes surrounded by obtuse halos, more than an eternity is required to see the shape or even the reflected shape of the Father himself. What other mind except that mind of the begotten Son would attempt such an observation of that shape of our Father, who art in Heaven, although John had the correct mindset when he wrote both in the spiritual and in the gigantic from Patmos. Yet his well-disciplined and apostolic mind was insufficient for the more than eternal task of the observation of the shape of the Father.

It is one thing to write the words, the sayings, and the teachings of Jesus, and to even record those amazing wonders and wonderful miracles performed by Him, but it is nearly impossible to observe the confidence and the dedication that He himself put forth in their accomplishments or for their manifestations. How confident to know that the works of Him that sent me actually do work and of having the knowledge that the works of God should be made manifest. When you are armed with this information, this knowledge, and with this confidence as Jesus was armed, you will then better understand His teachings, his confidence, and dedication in these words; Nothing shall be impossible unto you (Matt. 17:20).

There is one realization and observation that Jesus boasted of: as long as I am in the world, I am the light of the world (John 9:5). The population of the world nor of the activities of the world, whether they be earthly or heavenly, hold any meaning during the ministry of Jesus because all of the laws of nature and science were subjected to His defiance of them, and he defied them all.

Now John said, when he had thus spoken, He spat on the ground and made clay of the spittle, and He anointed the eyes of the blind man with the clay (John 9:6). What went on here was far greater than that which John portrayed of His works. After such a general and universal proclamation by Jesus, you should expect no less than He proclaims in this miraculous work done here. But why the eyes and not the ears of this man born blind, in Matthew 6:22 and Luke 11:34, Jesus saith, the light of the body is the eye. Here is a body that by nature had never seen light, not even the natural order of light. But it was not because of sin that this body had never seen even the natural order from light.

Let us now focus on this seemingly simple but great miracle performed by Jesus here. By nature, this body had never seen light of any kind, and it seemed that it was not in the least bit possible that he would ever see light had it not been for sin either. When you consider that the law of his body had excluded light from him, not ever with the possibility of him having vision were it not for sin, similar to the tree, which Jesus came upon, but found no fruit thereon (Matt. 21:19 and Mark 11:13). Jesus knew that God had the power to form whatsoever He wished (Gen. 2:7, 8, and 19). He knew further that according to Genesis 2:6–7, before anything is formed into any object having life, a mist or some form of water, His spittle or some form of moisture must be used, even in such a bleak circumstance as this man born blind, having his body void of light by nature. It is these natures, their laws, and their circumstances, which Jesus must overcome and overthrow. Therefore, when Jesus spat on the ground, He had to work the soil and dust into the exact consistency using His moist spittle with mixture and taking care that the mixture does not become too hardened, working this consistency with a power that only He and God knows for the moment.

Every physician knows that there are healing properties in spittle. But let us look further into this spittle of Jesus. In John 4:10, He promised that if thou wouldest have asked of Him, He would have given thee living waters, as those that Jesus possess. Everything that God put into nature in parts, He put into Jesus in whole, and that includes laws also. Therefore, the very same process that is required for the topological reaction of the planet earth to generate clay from sedimentation, from His own spittle, Jesus likewise made clay. But look further and more specifically; this clay from Jesus's spittle, unlike the spittle upon His face (Matt. 26:67), became the very fashion of eyes with sight and with the retention of sight. This is in spite of all the circumstances against the man's body, being born blind from his birth. Let us not forget that the works of God should be made manifest in Him also. Since the works of God should be made manifest (John 9:3) and greater works than these shall ye do (John 14:12), what then is the greatest manifestation in the history of the world? Being far greater than this work of God being made manifest? Is it not the manifestation of the Son of God through you (Rom. 8:19)? These are the works of God, having been made manifest by Him through you. Then are fulfilled these words of Jesus; I am come into this world that they which see not might see (John 9:39). Just as some creatures are linked to others for their lives, we are linked to Jesus for this manifestation of the Son of God.

Now there is a certain caliber of saints, which are revealed through the time of Christ Jesus only. Of all of those gods of antiquity among all of the world's nations, even of olden times, no other god among all of the world nations could ever proclaim this truth: All that ever came before me are thieves and robbers (John 10:8). Ancient myths and folklore are filled with gods, and the imagination of ancient nations has concocted encyclopedias of them, even carving woods and stones of them, worshipping mountains and trees and animals as gods. Some worship elements, fire, rivers, suns, moons, and stars. Some worship comets, asteroids, and rocks, and some others even worship this planet earth, other planets, and nature.

Therefore, all that ever came before me are thieves and robbers. I am come into this world that they, which see not, might see. This has nothing to do with the sheep themselves, for they know only His voice alone. This was the brilliant plan of predestination for them. Note that the sheep are known only through the shepherd. The ground is known to be wet when it rains upon it. Were you to compare the commandment of those granted to Jesus to those of the Old Testament granted to Moses, could you differentiate between the two, which is greatest, Exodus 20:3:17 or John 10:18? Commanding the fatherly power to lay your life down and to take it again far surpasses those of the olden standards of scripture and seems a world apart in their execution of them. Those commandments of the Old Testament savorest those things that be of men, while these commandments here savorest the things that be of God. You choose for yourself which has the greatest power.

Moses had already requested the ideal shepherd in Numbers 27:16–17 before Joshua was named and anointed before the congregation (Num. 27:19) and before Jesus made His proclamation (John 10:11). As to the evaluation of all those gods of antiquity and of their worth, Jesus boasts, my Father is greater than all (John 10:29). Here He doesn't mean that His Father is just greater than all gods alone, but that He is greater than the vision of all and everything else that exists.

If you were a Pharisee in the day of Jesus and had heard Him declare (John 10:34) as He walked in Solomon's porch at the Feast of Dedication (John 10:22–23), you would have been amazed to find that Jesus had not only included this writing of Psalm 8:26 with the law, seeing how they exclude every book from the law being the Pentateuch. He also exclusively declared, is it not written in your law, I said, ye are gods (John 10:34)? Almost as if He was telling them under this circumstance of godliness to also include the book of Psalms under their law. Otherwise, they would never hear this proclamation, I said, ye are gods, since they knew only the Pentateuch of Moses. Although ye are gods, and as gods, ye are the children of the most high God, yet none other can proclaim: I and my Father are one (John 10:30). Therefore, all that ever came before me are thieves and robbers. At the end of this episode when they sought again to take Him, He conveyed himself away out of their hands and went away again beyond Jordan.

Those of you who are keen on Jesus, who love both Him and His words, who believe in Him as He proclaim himself to be, who believe in His signs, wonders and miracles, and upon whose life He has had an effect, you can accept the distinction between John 8:12, I am the light of the world, and John 11:9, the light of this world, as these papers has proven all along.

We now arrive at another event in His ministry where you are asked to be the judge of what is revealed in this miraculous event to ascertain its truth. Some of you who visited the traditional site of the tomb of Lazarus located forty and two steps beneath ground level, on which Jesus stood, should have made these observations. Did anyone who visit the crypt beneath the ground take time to consider after reading this account of John in the eleventh chapter how Lazarus came forth at the bidding of Jesus? Of all the things that Jesus admitted to being in the book alone, He identifies more (John 11:25) and will identify and acclaim more (John 14:6 and John 14:1), and much more than this gospel (Rev. 22:13, Rev. 1:11, and Rev. 1:18).

If you remember Mark 3:13, He called unto Him whom He would, and they came unto Him. Remember how He goeth up onto a mountain through conveying Himself there and calling whom He would to levitate themselves there to Himself also? Well, there is no difference here with Lazarus either. He calleth whom He will, Lazarus in this calling forth, and he came to Him. Let us argue your case for the sake of truth. According to these writings of John, first of all, the body of Lazarus had begun to decompose and stink (John 11:39), for according to Jewish customs, when the soul leaves the body, it lingers around the body for three days before it makes its final departure from the body, leaving it to rot, decompose, and stink. But behold, if now the body of Lazarus had begun to decompose and stinketh, how can life reenter a decomposed body and live? According to John 12:1, Lazarus lived on. Therefore, one of two things had to occur when Jesus called Lazarus forth from the grave. Either Jesus had to speak words so purified with life and power in order to reverse the decomposition, or He had to actuate His own principle in Luke 5:38 and made Lazarus a new body for this new life.

There are biblical facts that those of you can consider about how Jesus operated under these circumstances. The crypt and burial place of Abraham, Ezekiel, David, and many others are well-known. When Jesus went down to hell to lead those captive away on the eventful morning of His resurrection, He did not send their spirits back into their old bodies, yet the graves were opened, and many bodies of the saints, who slept, arose (Matt. 27:52). He did not use their old bodies to resurrect their lives; therefore, He actuated His principle for the new when He raised Lazarus from the dead that the Son of God might be glorified thereby.

Now about the levitation of Lazarus after Jesus called him forth from his crypt, read Matthew 27:44 with visual understanding; and he that was dead came forth. Now you must observe how he came forth from beneath forty and two steps up through a narrow passageway. He came forth, bound hand and foot with grave clothes. Therefore, he could not walk up the steps nor balance himself up the narrow passageway because he was bound hand and foot with grave clothes. If further evidence is needed, and his face was bound with a napkin, therefore, he could not see where he was going nor could he walk because his feet were bound. He could not balance himself because his hands were bound, and he could not see because his face was bound with a napkin. Mummified, yet coming forth. Now for those who undressed Lazarus to make it appear as though he was freed to move about, you should closely read Jesus's instructions; loose him, and let him go. He was still fully bound while still standing before Jesus, and as usual, Jesus walked no more openly, but went away (John 11:54). Let the reader perceive how he went away. For those of you who wish to know and better understand the importance of drawing the mind and the teaching of the Pharisees to the Psalm as part of your law also (John 10:34), you may find the purpose of Jesus for this in Luke 24:44, that all things must be fulfilled, which was written in the law of Moses, of which they studied to master, and in the prophets, of which they did not study, and in the Psalms concerning me.

Thus, considering and studying only the Pentateuch could not give them the full knowledge of Jesus nor could they understand what other knowledge of Jesus that must be fulfilled by Him. If God sent forth knowledge of Jesus beyond those of the law of Moses in scriptures written after the law through the prophets and in Psalms concerning Jesus fulfilling them, and they had not read them, then Matthew 23:37 is more easily accepted as to why Jesus himself cried these words against them: O Jerusalem, Jerusalem, thou that kills the prophets and stones them which are sent unto thee. God sent them to further the knowledge of the fulfillment for Jesus himself. But since they knew only the Pentateuch, they could not accept anyone else, even though the prophets and Psalms were sent to them by God himself. They could not have answered the cry of Isaiah 53:1 unto the Lord.

How could they believe scriptures they had not read about or this further report to be fulfilled by Jesus? They could have never understood Matthew 11:13 nor would they have known how they were described in prophecy in Matthew 13:14 nor would they know the truth of Matthew 13:57, and herein is revealed the reasons why Jesus often asked them; did ye never read in the scriptures (Matt. 21:42 and Matt. 21:16), yea, have ye never read? How could they have read from the Psalms or the prophets if they rejected them and those who sent them, including John the Baptist? Now whether they rejected them or believed them or not, all things must be fulfilled, which were writing in the law of Moses, in the prophets, and in the Psalms concerning Jesus. And behold, the joy and the revelation of Luke 24:27.

For those of you who wish to know the error of the Sadducees in their application described by Jesus in Matthew 22:29, Jesus described their error in their lack of understanding of the power of God. You may turn to read Leviticus 20:21: And if a man shall take his brother's wife, it is an unclean thing; he hath uncovered his brother's nakedness; they shall be childless. So it was with the seven; the law itself does not change because of the error of the misinterpretation of it. When you are associated with your surroundings, things and people of the community become very familiar objects. Such was not the case with Jesus and those of Jerusalem although He was taken there every year at the Feast of the Passover by his parents (Luke 2:41).

After His Bar Mitzvah, He studied with a little known sect called the Essenes, which steered clear of those royalties at Jerusalem. When He rode into Jerusalem to fulfill the prophecy of Zechariah 9:9 with the cry of Psalms 118:26, all the city was moved, saying who is this (Matt. 20:10)? The Jerusalem community was alarmed because they heard that this Jesus, the prophet of Nazareth of Galilee, had called Lazarus out of his grave, as we have said and raised him from the dead (John 12:17).

Has anyone of you ever considered the monumental and the caustic strength of the transfiguration of the Lord and Savior Jesus Christ? First, you must consider from the initial accounts (Matt. 17:1, Mark 9:2, and Luke 9:28) how he went into the mountain with the apostles, and as the adversary had taken Him into a high mountain (Matt. 3:8), showed Him all the kingdoms of the world, the glory of them, and He now has chosen an adversary (John 6:70); He now bringeth them up into a high mountain apart (Matt. 17:1), but He did not bring up Judas, revealing that His ways are not the ways of the world. For the prince of this world cometh and hath nothing in me (John 14:30).

If the church and the world would take note: Jesus would do nothing of Himself, as we all know (John 8:28). It has not yet been revealed to me by the Lord why Jesus would bring up Peter onto this mountain, return and take up James while leaving Peter there in the mountain, and then leaving Peter and James on the mountain, He would return and take up John into the mountain lastly. The purpose for these three transports onto the mountain, carrying them individually, may not be for the understanding of the minds of this world, but be assured that this purpose was in the plan of the Father first before Jesus carried it out. If you can, consider that Peter is rock, and that James and John are Boanerges (Mark 3:17) or Sons of Thunder. These very three Jesus did surname apart from the rest of them to serve some binding purpose, and they were always together (Mark 5:37, Mark 13:3, Mark 14:33, Luke 5:10, and Luke 8:51). These three would be surnamed because they would be the gates of the foundation into the apostleship. A rock and Sons of Thunder. This is why Jesus took meticulous care in bringing each of them onto this mountain apart. But we spoke of the monumental aspects of His transfiguration and the spiritual strength required to fully comprehend all component parts of it, which none has fully done, and I am no guarantee either. But we do know that the chief apostle is here and that the other two making up the gate of the foundation into the apostleship is here. We know that Jesus himself is here also. Now at the same time these are here, Moses is here with them. Elijah is here also, and Moses and Elijah are sent with a message for Jesus (Luke 9:31), speaking of His decrease, which He should accomplish at Jerusalem.

To reveal the scope that would cause Moses and Elijah to be manifested to Jesus would extend beyond the reach of these papers. But you should be familiar with the history and life of Moses and Elijah and the circumstances surrounding their own departure from earth (Deut. 32:49–50), but in particular to Deuteronomy 34:6 and in 2 Kings 2:11.

No man knew where Moses was buried, and no man knew where Elijah went into Heaven. And although hundreds of years separate them, here and now, they come to Jesus with the same message. But rest assured that this principle of Jesus (John 6:44) is still in operation. No man can come to me, except the Father, which hath sent me, draw him. The shining of His face likened unto that of Moses (Exod. 34:29), the cause of His raiment to gleam. Then here is the presence of the Father (Matt. 17:5); this is my beloved Son, in whom I am well pleased; hear ye Him. Truly a monumental association at this transfiguration.

It is good to hear the voice of God coming from between two cherubim above the mercy seat exemplifying the nation that made the mercy seat (Exod. 25:22), but it is better to hear the voice of God coming from Heaven above the earth for the world, wherein no nation can make claim to have made exemplifying God (John 12:28). And this was done in request to the response of Jesus, to which He would reply, this voice came not because of me but for your sakes (John 12:30) that the world may know that in spite of Jesus being on earth, there is a God in Heaven that does glorify. It is bad that those who heard this voice (John 12:29) did not comprehend Jesus's interpretation of its purpose and meaning.

The study of astrobiological life of any sort within the universe anywhere would also come under this law of Christ Jesus of John 12:25; he that loveth his life shall lose it, and he that hateth his life in this world shall keep it until life eternal. You may ask the question, how can alien beings within other parts of the universe come to love their lives? The rule would be applied no differently elsewhere within the universe than is already applied upon the earth. That is, pride in association with wealth within the social structure of life whether it is astrophysical, astrocelestial, biological, astrobiological, cosmological, or terrestrial pride in association with any system of wealth that is maintained, hardens any creature to life of whatever form or location. Do not forget Matthew 6:19: Lay not up for yourselves treasures upon earth where moth and rust doth corrupt and where thieves break through and steal. Many throughout history have lost their lives while protecting their treasures from such corruption and thieves. This universal law of Jesus holds true for all creatures of life anywhere within the physical universe, and that rule is: he that hateth his life in this world, shall keep it unto live eternal. Forget not Matthew 16:26; for what is a man profited if he shall gain the whole world and lose his own soul? He has profited nothing. Neither has any other creature than man, should they possess a soul. Judgment is pronounced upon this world (John 12:31), and the prince of this world is cast out (John 12:31). Why then should you lose your soul for it?

Take note of how Jesus described the departure after His discourse and instructions for believing in the light (John 12:36). Jesus not only conveyed himself away but he also vanished out of their sight, hiding himself from them.

Be aware that none of you truly know the meaning, the true meaning, of the Son of Man and the relationship of this act of Jesus in the instruction of believing in the light, that ye may be the children of light (John 12:36), and then conveying himself away and vanishing immediately thereafter. Light is to be seen. So then after such a revelation on light, why should He vanish and not be seen? The reason lieth in this purpose. The Son of Man must be lifted up (John 12:34). I must ask your faith in these papers to believe in what God has shown me of such matters that I write.

The origin about the nature and being of the Son of Man began as a plan of God himself before the Garden of Eden and after the creation of Adam. What now is about to be revealed takes nothing from the claims of Jesus himself, but it does take the reader to understand things of why the very ancient compilers of the Holy Bible took their course of the description of things therein for the sake of the lack of their understanding of them.

Now to reach across the history of time and back into the days of Eden and its human occupants, namely Adam and Eve, and to come upon the plan of God for His purpose for their lives, requires the knowledge and leading of God himself.

The plan of God for Eve was exactly the plan, which He carried out for the Virgin Mary. His former plan, which was His original plan (Luke 1:35), was that the Holy Ghost shall come upon Eve, and the power of the highest shall overshadow thee. Therefore, the holy thing, which shall be born of thee, shall be called the Son of God, first. Then after that, ye shall know your husband Adam, and that fleshly thing which shall be born of thee shall be called the Son of Man. This is, this was, and this plan of God was not to be changed. But when God returned to the garden to execute His original plan, He was met with these words from Eve; the serpent beguiled me, and I fell (Gen. 3:13). The ancient compilers of the Bible thought that this was too graphic for the populace. Therefore, Jesus came as the original plan of God to be carried out for both the Son of God and for the Son of Man. Truly, the hour has come that the Son of Man should be glorified (John 12:23).

Now if so much can be done by the Son of Man, a child of Adam after the original plan without interruption by the serpent, how much more can be done by the Son of God, which Jesus exemplified, had He not had to carry forth also that nature of the Son of Man? Would not this give you the power to vanish as the Son of God? But as sons of men, ye are the light of the world (Matt. 5:14), and as the Son of God, all power is given unto you in heaven and in earth (Matt. 28:18). Take note of why Jesus saith, now is the Son of Man glorified, and God is glorified in Him (John 13:31) finally. The enemy is now acting within his own nature and element (John 13:30). He is at this time not in the position to thwart the Son of Man from being glorified, and the nature of that magnificent glorification is concealed from the eyes of man to behold. These entities are the natures of Jesus hidden away from the world.

Consider who the Son of Man is according to this definition, and consider why He is now glorified (John 13:31) under the circumstance of the absence of the enemy. If the enemy had not been first in the beguiling of Eve in the Garden of Eden, the first Son of the Man, Adam, instead of Cain his firstborn, would have been glorified, instead of being a vagabond and fugitive (Gen. 4:14) in the earth. God would have been glorified in him, but instead God said, now art thou cursed from the earth (Gen. 4:11). Compare Genesis 4:16 with John 13:30. Both Cain and Judas went out from the presence of the Lord, and God himself could not have been glorified in either one of them. Here is an understanding of Jesus that is prerequisite to this Son of Man that is also prerequisite to His nature that no one has as yet comprehended.

If God be glorified in Him, which is a prerequisite of God himself being glorified in Him according to the working of His original plan to bring about the Son of Man by Adam then the original plan was not forfieted. If God be glorified in that Son of Man, then God shall also glorify Him in himself. Within these prerequisites of Jesus on this subject matter, there are revelations of God, which astounds the mind to which these things are revealed. For God would take into himself as He also did with Enoch (Gen. 5:24) this Son of Man in order to show Him His own glory and shall straightway glorify Him. This would be done because He is the Son of Man. It is good to know God in such ways as His ways. God would glorify the Son of Man in himself and would be glorified. This godly method of procreation would last forevermore because there could never be any such thing as death or decay. I would remind the reader that there are many such ways with God, with whom all things are possible. According to the prophecies of Jesus (Luke 17:22), the days will come when ye shall desire to see one of the days of the Son of Man, and ye shall not see it. Therefore, take note; even thus shall it be in the day, when the Son of Man is revealed (Luke 17:30).

Beholding the wonderful ways of God is a great opportunity very few humans seldom obtain. Here is also a great opportunity very few humans seldom obtain or are offered to obtain. After Jesus descended the mountain and conveyed himself into Capernaum, it does not matter which account you accept (Matt. 8:5 or Luke 7:1) or any other written report obtainable, the seldom known opportunity among humans is that the centurion of the written accounts believing Jesus to prove Psalm 107:20 for the healing of his servant caused Jesus to marvel (Matt. 8:10 and Luke 7:9). Indeed, this rarity is seldom known among humans, who are always most amazed at the words, the acts, the signs, and the wonders of Jesus. Anyone else needing a more specific knowledge about the Son of Man may read it as it is written in the law of the Lord (Luke 2:23 and Lev. 12:2).

We now present a rarity of the present, which should not, according to the promise of Jesus, lay outside of the grasp of all believers in Him. According to the words of truth spoken by Jesus himself, written with seeming disbelief to the believers in Him, "Verily, verily I say unto you, He that believeth on me, the works that I do, shall he do also." You may say that this statement of promise, which is built upon the faith in Jesus, explains all of those works of Jesus, which are being done by the believers in the church. Maybe all believers are performing the works of Jesus at rates far too alarming for me to behold, but if such works of Jesus are being carried out by believers, I myself wish that they would slow them down so that I may bear witness to the truth of them as Jesus would have it. All I know is that Jesus presents the proof of himself through His exact works to those who believe in Him. These proofs are not difficult to prove by believers, even as the proof of those who also believe in Him as the scripture has said, by rivers of living waters flowing from within their own belly. In other words, believe in Him, and these works of His will come forth. Then you will prove for yourself through these works whether Jesus could levitate and convey himself away. Of course, according to John (John 21:25), there are also many other things that Jesus did, that if they should be written, every one, I suppose, that even the world itself could not contain the books that should be written. Now in light of John 14:12, "the works that I do, shall he do also" and John 21:25, "and there are also many other things, which Jesus did" means that doing many other things that Jesus did, the likes of which if they should be written, every one, I suppose, said John that even the world in light of you the believer doing them yourself, could not contain the books that should be written. If you can understand the essence of Jesus and the meaning of the writing of John about many other unwritten things that Jesus did, verily I say unto you, if ye have faith and doubt not, ye shall not only do this and all other things, which is done to the fig tree, but also, if ye shall say unto the mountain, be thou removed and be thou cast into the sea, it shall be done (Matt. 21:21). Nothing shall be impossible unto you, the believer.

My fear is that you, the believer, do not yet comprehend the essence and magnitude, which are on display here. First, to do all of the written works of Jesus recorded within and by the gospels, confirmed unto us by them that heard and saw Him do them, and secondly, besides confirming to us those things, which both Matthew and John heard Jesus say, do. John admits that there are also many other things, which Jesus did, which were beyond the scope of the gospels. It is also these many other things, which Jesus did, which are beyond the scope of the four gospels, which the believer must do likewise. You may ask this question as a believer in the Lord Jesus: how can I also do many other things that Jesus did if they are not recorded within the gospels? Well, according to John 14:12, Jesus promised: verily, verily I say unto you, he that believeth on me, the works that I do, whether they are written within the gospels or not, shall he do also. A great promise that is to be fulfilled because Jesus cannot lie, and besides, according to His own will, God himself bore witness to those who confirmed the works of Jesus to us with signs and wonders, with diverse miracles and with gifts of the Holy Ghost. These things were done so that there should be no doubt to the true believer. Where are the doers of the written and recorded works of Jesus? Have they done such great works of Jesus that they are now doing many other things that Jesus did and are now operating in some invisible media beyond the scope of the gospels or the church?

In the days of Matthew and John, the two chosen (Matt. 9:9 and Matt. 4:21), who confirmed unto us those many written things that Jesus did, God bore them witness according to His own will while Jesus was yet with them (Mark 6:12–13 and 6:30), and even afterward (Mark 16:20). Did faith stop there? Are there yet no believers according to John 14:12? What about many other things that Jesus did that should be written besides the gospels? This brings us to the third category of the works of Jesus. First, there are those <u>written works</u>, which He did that are recorded in the gospels. Second, there are the <u>many other things</u>, which Jesus did that should be written. Then thirdly, there are those <u>greater works</u> than these (John 14:12). Again I ask you, where are they? Where is he that believeth in me? For when you search the church and the world, surely you will find him that believeth in Jesus in full operation in these works of the gospel and beyond, the Lord working with them and confirming the word with signs following (Mark 16:20). In other words, you who truly believe in Jesus has this mindset: I must work the works of Him that sent me while it is day (John 9:4), and you may not have time to read or study these Jesus papers because of your works beyond the gospels and the world.

Do not forget that even the world itself could not contain the books that should be written (John 21:25). If you stand out upon the earth in your outstanding amazement, beyond those that are recorded in the gospels, remember this verbal description of Jesus, "A city that is set on a hill cannot be hid" (Matt. 5:14). And if you are the light of the world, so that even the world itself could not contain the books that should be written, according to John 14:12, by doing the same works of Jesus, surely you also fulfill these words of Jesus. The righteous shine forth as the sun in the kingdom of their Father (Matt. 13:43), and your legacy far exceeds that legacy of John (John 5:35) and identify you with the legacy of supremacy (1 John 1:5); God is Light. Now should the reader also wish to relate the exceeding works far beyond the legacy of John (John 5:35), He was a burning and a shining light; he need read only to the next verse (John 5:36) to identify the greater witness and the works which Jesus himself announces. Jesus announces that the works, which the believers also do, bear greater witness than that of John (John 5:36). Greater works, greater witness.

EVEN GREATER WORKS

NOW LET US STEP many, many light years ahead of the present world in lieu of John 21:25, and there are also many other things that Jesus did, that if they should be written every one, I suppose that even the world itself could not contain the books that should be written. These things the gospels do not record and greater works than these shall He do, which the gospels also do not record (John 14:12). If I may add, what possible greater works than Jesus can any believer do? It must be known that he or she must first do the works of Jesus first, grace for grace. But how far do the works of Jesus transcribe and are they transcribed according to His definition and purpose?

The many other unwritten things that Jesus did, which are not recorded within the four gospels are also not recorded within the epistles. And the book of the Revelation of Jesus Christ merely cloak great visionary works of Jesus, which are beyond the broad bands of human understanding to execute, or so they seem to be. If there also are works of Jesus, according to John 1:3, all things were made by Him, and without Him was not anything made, that was made; and that is whether they are great visionary works or not, all were thus simply works of Jesus included in the great work of the creation of all known things, written or not. As we leave the world light years in arrears, with the believers constantly astounding it with those great works of Jesus that they do, with God also bearing them witness, both with signs and wonders and with diverse miracles and gifts of the Holy Ghost, according to His own will (Heb. 2:4); let us move on to those greater works than these, which are further being offered by Jesus himself to capture God's greater witnessing, both with signs and wonders and with diverse miracles and gifts of the Holy Ghost, still according to His own will.

These greater works of Jesus are to be accomplished by believers of Him, some who say that they believe in Him out of the world, Jesus promised that there are (John 16:27) and shall be believers (John 17:20), the greater works to be accomplished by them, stand out beyond reaching one-sixth of the world's population at one time through television and satellite as some suppose such to be the case with the gospel.

In the first place, greater works than the present works of Jesus would raise your work standard to those standards of the angels and beyond. This is because He was made a little lower than the angels, who are greater than man the believer. Some would consider Acts 2:41 to be a greater work because of the number that was added to them. Let's consider the great multitude of them that believed when considering the very works of Jesus to be done in Acts 4:32 and Acts 5:14. You may also consider the fame that spread throughout the cities around Jerusalem after the apostle Peter conveyed his shadow over their streets while healing them (Acts 5:16) although he, because of the multitude, passed over the heads of the people in his transport, so that at the least, his shadow passing by might overshadow some of them (Acts 5:15). This still was not a greater work than those of Jesus, of which He promised (John 14:12). Even it was not a greater work than those of Jesus when He walked on the water to go to Jesus (Matt. 14:29) and least we forget the powers of the angels, which are above those of men (2 Pet. 2:11) and others.

Let us view some of the works of angels as are biblically recorded. They guard the way of the Tree of Life (Gen. 3:24), which is a great work; they appeared as three personages (Gen. 18:2) to Abraham and destroyed Sodom and Gomorrah (Gen. 32:32). With Moses, there are acts of angels, with Joshua, with the parents of Samson, David, and others. In the New Testament era, angels that are greater in power did many wonderful works, whereas some, the apostles themselves could have done, being given so much power (Matt. 10:1, Matt. 10:8, Acts 2:4, and Acts 4:31). Observe the work of the angel of the Lord in Acts 5:19 when he opened the prison doors and brought forth the twelve apostles on this event. He brought them forth under his power, not theirs. Observe the works of the angels done by the angel of Acts 12:9 and Acts 12:10 before vanishing before the apostle Peter's sight (Acts 12:10). If you desire to know what angels are and why they are sent forth for heirs of salvation, please read Hebrews 1:14. They are sent forth to minister for them, who shall be heirs of salvation.

Now you come to greater works of angels of greater capacities for greater works. In the book of the Revelation of Jesus Christ, you will find Jesus identifying himself to mighty angels whose works are over the authority of churches: Ephesus, Smyrna, Pergamos, Thyatira, Sardis, Philadelphia, and Laodicea (Rev. 1:11). Observe the works of the angels standing on the four corners of the earth holding the four winds of the earth (Rev. 7:1). Observe the angel whose work is to carry the seal of the living God (Rev. 7:2), the mighty angel whose work is to proclaim the end of time (Rev. 10:6), the angel whose work is to cast out the enemy from Heaven (Rev. 12:9), the angel whose work is to preach His everlasting gospel (Rev. 14:6). Also observe the angel whose works have power over fire (Rev. 14:18), angels whose works are to administer plagues (Rev. 5:1), the work of the angel to scorch men (Rev. 16:8), the angel whose works are with vials (Rev. 17:1), the angel whose works are proclamation (Rev. 18:1), the mighty angel whose work is with the millstone (Rev. 18:21), the work of the binding angel (Rev. 20:2), or the last of the working angels, the twelve protective angels at the gates (Rev.

21:12). There can be no doubt that these working angels have works and statures fitted for their tasks and labors before God alone.

Now there were great works among the holy apostles that are recorded by Luke in the book of the Acts of the Apostles. There were many amazing moments also in Acts 1:9, after Jesus promised them more power, having already given them power before for their ministries (Matt. 10:1 and Matt. 10:8), He was taken up. They were to receive power again after Acts 2:2 in Acts 4:31, and the apostle Peter would witness Acts 2:4 and again in Caesarea in Acts 11:15. The crowd, having received Jesus out of their sight (Acts 1:9) and after their visitation of the two angels (Acts 1:10), they would return to tarry in the upper room, where the Holy Ghost would first be poured upon them (Acts 2:4). It would also be here in the upper room where prayer was being offered up by the other apostles and saints for Peter and John that the Holy Ghost would again attend to them (Acts 4:31).

There were wonders of amazing proportions done by the apostles (Acts 2:43, 3:11, 4:13, 4:33, 5:12, and 5:16). These wonders were performed before the apostle Peter would witness the third outpouring of the Holy Ghost in Caesarea (Acts 11:15). But of all these great signs, wonders, and miracles of diverse kinds, none have fit John 14:12 of works greater than those of Jesus, of which He himself said that he that believeth shall do.

All of those great works of signs and wonders, which are recorded throughout the Holy Bible and miracles of great proportions from books of other world religions and their belief systems, can simply compare with, if ye shall say unto this mountain be thou removed, and be thou cast into the sea, it shall be done (Matt. 21:21). How can your frail mind handle Mount Everest being moved across the sky and hurled into the sea at your command?

It would be difficult for the mind of Moses to phantom the parting of the Red Sea at the raising of his rod (Exod. 14:16), without God first conditioning his mind beforehand in preparation for the event, as well as being prepared for the Mount Sinai visitation (Exod. 19:18).

What then can actually prepare the frail mind to receive acts of greater works, that of their magnificence would be of the magnitude of the glorification seen by Jesus himself to measure them beyond His ordinary works, which are known and written in the gospels and of the many other things that He did, that even the world itself could not contain the books that would be written (John 21:25)? Apparently these are grater works that can actually be done and accomplished by the believers. What is significant about the four gospels is that neither they nor the book of the Acts of the Apostles nor the epistles, and this also includes the book of the Revelation of Jesus Christ, describes greater works done by anyone found within the pages of their covers. If you think that because the two witnesses of Revelation 11:3–11, having such great power and had more works than those of Jesus, I would only refer you back to John 1:3, which included them also.

Greater works mean understanding greater realities with greater capabilities to perform them. If the principle of Jesus still holds true here, for without me ye can do nothing (John 15:5), then these greater works that are to be done by believers according to John 14:12, cannot be done without Jesus either. Therefore, on what level are you looking at and believing in Jesus?

This statement proves that Jesus is greater than those moments of His performance of signs and wonders and diverse miracles, and Jesus himself knew of these power reserves. In John 5:20, He said, "He will show Him greater works than these that ye may marvel, and these greater works do bear witness of Himself." He said, "For the works, which the Father hath given me to finish, the same works that I do, bear witness of me, that the Father hath sent me (John 5:36)." Thus, the greater works would bear greater witness also, that the Father has also sent you, if being here within the world requires proof of that.

Before we reveal the greatest possible works or work of the Holy Bible, being the greatest of the greater works than those done by Jesus himself, even according to John 21:25, there are also many other things that Jesus did, which if they should be written every one, I suppose that even the world itself could not contain the books that should be written. The gospels have already recorded some of the works of Jesus, which according to John, there are also many other things that Jesus did, some of which we have shown you in that they are not properly recorded in the gospels to be understood by most of today. This revelation is no private interpretation of the scripture. We will first unveil many great teachings of Jesus to the world and church.

If only those of the church would accept the teachings of Jesus and those other things that he introduced into the world for those of His church for which He gave His holy and righteously begotten life, then the whole world and its worldly order, as well as the total nature of things, would change right before the very eyes of the whole world. This does not mean that the believers do not receive eternal life through Christ for there are scriptures, many spoken by Jesus himself that verifies their guarantee (John 11:26, 6:58, 6:47, 6:50, 6:54, 6:40, 5:24, 4:36, 3:16), and other scriptures.

Jesus left a knowledge behind that even the apostles themselves could not interpret. For how can you or anyone else interpret the knowledge of even the comforter, armed with the capacity and the eternal energy to comfort and abide forever? With their finite senses, how could they or even you, the reader, interpret eternity?

Now what does it mean to have a being given to you who has the capacity to abide with you forever (John 14:16)? How would you interpret this prayer of the promise of Jesus being answered in the finite meeting the infinite? It is this kind of knowledge of Jesus that the church does not pursue although it ought to because it predicates the believer personally and is the only recipient qualified to prepare for such a meeting and union, much like those qualified in Acts 2:4, from the promise of Luke 24:49, when one part of the prayer of Jesus from John 14:16 was fulfilled.

This infinite met the finite, and the results may be read in Acts 2:1–13 with a prophecy reflected from early scripture, which was spoken by the prophet Joel. Since we are into the greater things, compare Acts 2:16 with Acts 11:16 for the greatest memory of the apostle Peter about the same Holy Ghost in Acts 11:15, as was in Acts 2:1–4. Only this time, it was not among the Jews at Jerusalem, but it was of people of another nation (Acts 10:28). The same Holy Ghost effect as was in Jerusalem (Acts 11:15) shows proof of that was at the beginning (Acts 2:4), and the words of Jesus are greater than the words of the prophet Joel (Joel 2:28).

But wait, we speak of the finite meeting the infinite where we have already observed two national effects; that of the Jews (Acts 2:4) and that of the Italian band (Acts 11:15) with no other nation laying claim except the Samaritans (Acts 8:17), the Ethiopian Eunuch (Acts 8:39), and it is of great interest to the reader who may have doubted the report of the effect of the baptism upon Jesus in Matthew 3:16. When He was baptized, He went up straightway out of the water. By comparing this exact effect upon Philip in Acts 8:39, the Spirit of the Lord caught Philip, proving John 14:12, the works that I do, shall He do also. Of course, all works are done by the Father, whether they be lesser, greater, or the greatest. The Pisidians (Acts 13:52) lay claim, the Ephesians (Acts 19:6) also lay claim, but since Acts 17:26 hold all nations under one blood, all of them can lay claim. That is of the finite meeting infinite on the international level, and He still maintains the capacity to abide with you forever.

Now about the power of having an infinite comforter who may abide with you forever, Jesus also promised the believer, who is justified from all things, according to Acts 13:39 from which He could not be justified by the law, the spirit of truth.

Here now is a distinction that the world cannot receive. And how much of a distinction is it? Consider the distinction of Genesis 1:26, where God said, "Let us make man in our own image, after our likeness, and let them have dominion over the fish of the sea, and over the fowl of the air." Now compare the distinction of Matthew 6:26, where Jesus admonished, "Behold the fowls of the air, for they sow not, neither do they reap, nor gather into barns; yet your heavenly Father feedeth them. Are ye not much better than they? You have dominion over them, because you are much better than they, and it is your heavenly Father that feedeth them, over whom you have dominion." Man has lost that distinction and is embarrassed by the fowls of the air. Yet the world seems unable to neither comprehend nor grasp that distinction. As in John 17:17; thy word is truth, man lives not by bread only (Deut. 8:3). Having this distinction over the fowls of the air seems lost to the world, or rather it is lost to the world. As the world cannot receive, unless by some monumental and divine miracle, their distinction of dominance away from those shown by Jesus (Matt. 6:26) will continue to be embarrassed by all of its creatures in comparing their acts of labor with that of man, who sows and reaps and gathers into barns.

The world is thrown into a more profound state of chaos at this revelation of Jesus that the world cannot receive the spirit of truth. You may ask the question, by what then does the world verify its truth if it cannot receive the spirit of truth? The world cannot receive the spirit of truth in all of its magnificence, and we can see them from this, another reason for the rejection of Jesus in Matthew 4:8, after being shown all the kingdoms of the world and the glory of them, but not subject to the spirit of truth. Since the world cannot receive Him, can He be in operation in spite of this world's rejection? According to Jesus, the believer knows what the world cannot see, and He also knows what the world knoweth not (John 14:17). Because of the believer having this knowledge, He dwelleth with you and shall be in you because the true worshippers shall worship the Father in spirit and in truth (John 4:23).

This truth is verified in John 17:25: O righteous Father, the world hath not known thee. The most important things are unknown to the worlds, which are meant for the world, <u>and this is life</u>. Water is found all over Heaven in one form or another. Life's key ingredient and conditions for life is not found favorable for life all over Heaven.

If you live in this world, you can identify with your life, but you cannot identify with the spirit of your life as Genesis 6:3 states: My spirit shall not always strive with man. This is because His spirit of truth, whom the world cannot receive, is given life through grace by you, the believer. You, the believer, are His litmus paper, empowering you more spiritually as you decrease in worldly conditions. Very much like what's written in John 3:30, "He must increase, but I must decrease." John being in the position to you as the world or the personal pronoun, I, as the world must decrease, in relation to your association with it as a believer of Christ Jesus.

All churchgoing believers have heard or read, have taught or have preached the declarations of blessedness made by Jesus in His famous Sermon on the Mount near the Sea of Galilee. Though a church was built on the traditional site, still none have considered the transport nor power used by Jesus before He began His sermon proper (Matt. 5:1). Seeing the multitudes, He first conveyed himself up onto a mountain and surely that traditional site of the Sermon on the Mount by the Sea of Galilee cannot be classified as a mountain as described by Matthew 5:1, and viewed from the Sea of Galilee to the northwest, there are higher mountains than the mount of the traditional site of His famous sermon. Therefore, when seeing the multitudes, He went up onto a mountain. This mountain then was not the place of His famous sermon because the place of His traditional site, though it is a mount above the Sea of Galilee, is not a mountain according to Matthew, who witnessed, wrote, and participated in what was to follow when he finally was set.

Now therefore, when Matthew saw and recorded the experience of Jesus conveying himself up onto a mountain of which he did not identify for some unknown reason since he was an educated man in the state of the art tax collecting, wherein certain vicinities paid different taxations, unless that mountain onto which Jesus conveyed himself was beyond the boundary of his collection of taxes, and the name of that mountain held no interest to him. Therefore, seeing the multitudes, His going up onto a mountain was sufficient.

It must have been a notable sight to the multitudes to behold Jesus being conveyed again and again into the mountains (Mark 3:13 and Matt. 5:1), across the opened blue skies displaying such heavenly powers. When finally He finished his task in that mountain, as He would often pray (Luke 6:12), He would then come to the traditional site of the mount. When He was set, another display of His wonderful power was about to be exhibited again (Mark 3:13), they came unto Him. Also, see Matthew 10:1 when He called unto Him, His twelve disciples, they came unto Him. Then He opened his mouth and taught them.

The church has heard from the scripture, the Father speak on the approval of Jesus in verifying Him as His Son (Matt. 3:17 and Matt. 17:15). The church has heard from scripture, the Father speak on the glorification of Jesus (John 12:28). But now the church can hear from the Son what the Father speaks on loving and keeping not His sayings; he that loveth me not, keepeth not my sayings (John 14:24). Jesus said, "And the word, which ye hear is not mine, but the Father's, who sent me."

Now what do these binding words of the Father about His sayings mean? In their Fatherly meaning, their interpretation is that, if it is not within you to love me, it cannot be within you to keep my sayings either. But if a man keep my saying, he shall never see death (John 8:51), Jesus confirms.

Jesus learned the words of John 14:23; If a man love Me, he will keep my words, from John 14:24: He that loveth me not keepeth not my sayings (John 14:24).

The works of the Holy Ghost in John 14:26 teach comforting and bring all spoken things to remembrance by comparing spiritual things with spiritual things (1 Cor. 2:13) as He operates within the believer.

Because the natural man receives not the things of the Spirit of God, they being foolishness to him, it is not difficult to discern or interpret those things taught by Jesus for our learning, doctrine, practice, and works.

Jesus is the Savior of the world; therefore, nothing worldly is impossible to Him. When He speaks, being the Savior of the world to whom nothing is impossible, not only does He speak that which seems impossible but many times He also speaks that which is only natural to His understanding and which seems impossible to man. This is because He alone is the Savior of the world, and that authority cannot be shared by any other. The same principle may be applied to His works. His works are not of this world; therefore, no work is impossible to Him by which spirit the apostle exclaimed (Phil. 4:13), and when He works, being the Savior of the world to whom no work is impossible; not only does He work that which seems impossible, but oftentimes, He works that which is only natural to His understanding (John 14:10) but which seems impossible to man.

Take note of how Jesus testified in John 14:30: The prince of this world hath nothing in me. He is void of anything of the prince of this world (Matt. 4:8). The Savior of the world meets the prince of the world, but the prince of the world is not the Savior of the world and has nothing of the prince of the world within himself. Yet the prince of the world offers the Savior of the world all the kingdoms of the world and the glory of them.

When Jesus said, "I am the true vine, and my Father is the husbandman" (John 15:1), He speaks the knowledge of the linkage of things in general as well as specifically. See how you, the believer, are able to prove this claim in John 12:46, as the way out of darkness (John 4:10). The stretch unto everlasting life (John 4:10), His reach unto living water (John 4:14), His guiding into everlasting life (John 4:23), His leading into the knowledge of the true worshippers (Matt. 5:3–11), His stretching to reveal the blessedness to us (Matt. 7:13) reaching to reveal to us the entry into the strait gate (Matt. 6:33), reaching to reveal our first choice (Luke 21:11), reaching to take us beyond great earthquakes (Luke 21:25), reaching to take us beyond signs in the sun and in the moon and in the stars even (Luke 21:27), growing onward to show us the Son of Man in a cloud with power and great glory (John 14:6), and reaching to show that no man cometh unto the Father but by Him. Thus, it is an approved claim that He is the true vine, the Father is the husbandman, and ye are the branches.

THE VIRTUE OF JESUS

NOW THE WORLD AND those that dwell therein do not know many important things as on the occasion when Jesus questioned with sarcasm the Sanhedrin judge in John 3:12. If I have told you earthly things, and ye believe not, how shall ye believe if I tell you of heavenly things? And if they hate Him without a cause who came to offer the world solutions for every need, how then could they receive solutions for its every need, hating Him without a cause, who has every solution?

He made the world; the world knew Him not. He came unto His own; His own received Him not. They hate Him without a cause (John 15:25). You cannot know this from the Son (Luke 6:17–19), wherein when He came down with the holy apostles from the mountain and stood in the open plain of all Judaea and Jerusalem, and from the sea coast of Tyre and Sidon, which came to hear Him. A most wonderful sight to behold is Jesus and the apostles' astounding the multitudes below as they came down by the power of His spirit, unaware that they were about to witness like a burst of gamma rays from the explosion of a supernova on earth, a most luminous Jesus as He pulsated and radiated away, great power and virtue and healed them all. Should there be further doubt about this most luminous ability of Jesus, read the report of the apostle Paul in Acts 26:13. A light from Heaven above the brightness of the noonday sun. This report would bring us into an out of the world realm, which the world cannot receive. This revelation is not according to my own understanding, but it is by the word of the Lord Jesus himself (John 14:17).

If the believer can grasp this luminous display of Jesus, who is the word made flesh and by whom the worlds were framed (Heb. 11:3) and accept that these papers are about the Jesus of the Holy Bible who said that the world cannot receive the spirit of truth, when once we enter into that realm far beyond the world of the cosmos and universe, the very words of Jesus in John 14:17 about the spirit of truth will be proven without any doubt whatsoever.

Would Jesus's definition of the world include a neutron star that is ten miles in radius weighing in at one billion tons for each teaspoon of its matter? Even at one billion tons per atom, the fact remains that it was He who created the world that He defines, and no amount of weight, heat, mass, or velocity of the world's agenda would cause Him to change his definition of that which He created or thought to create, whether there are worlds or greater worlds having similar magnitudes of those worlds present.

Now before we delve into the place from whence worlds come and from which the world cannot receive, we would also offer a broad biblical perspective on the content of that virtue that emanated from Jesus on that day (Luke 6:19) and relate to the beasts of Revelation 13, which caused all the world to wonder (Rev. 13:3). From where did such beasts receive such great power to heal and to raise the dead and to cause all the world to wonder? One entry into understanding such a question, at least in part, may be derived from these related scriptures (John 6:70, Matt. 10:1 and 8), of whom a certain one among them in John 6:70 could not have cast out unclean spirits, according to Matthew 12:26, releasing such spirits into the world, having the power to heal, as did one of the beast of Revelation 13 and in Matthew 10:8, having power to raise from the dead the image of the beast of Revelation 13:15. The great explanations intertwined within these revelations would consume vast knowledge in writing them down in the pages of these Jesus papers, but suffice it to say that they are related, as all the works of the Holy Bible are related in their issues and whatever power anything or any creature may have or possess, whether as a consequence or by inheritance from the Holy Ghost. There is no power but of God, and the powers that be are ordained by God (Rom. 13:1), and this includes those having power also of Revelation 13.

Lest we forget those major and monumental observations to be put forth by these Jesus papers, we will reiterate them to refresh the mind of the believer. When both observations are taken, the first is what greater works than those done by Jesus can the believer do or what is the greatest work that the believer in Jesus can do? Second is what realm are we to enter into from which worlds emerged, the substance of which the world cannot receive being itself beyond the world according to Jesus?

The present process of fusion maintains the burning of the sun and stars as a gas, which will eventually burn themselves out, becoming as black as a sackcloth of hair (Rev. 6:12). According to today's discoveries within the heavens, after God made two great lights and set them in the firmament of the Heaven (Gen. 1:16–17), He went on and made and set many more, greater lights of suns, moons, stars, and more by the thousands and millions.

Now the things of which we speak are contained within the heavens themselves by the thousands. Nevertheless, it remains that the world cannot receive the spirit of truth, however magnificent it may be seen in its array and awe-inspiring glory.

It is only fair to alert the reader of the change of order from the consignee, seeing that as great and universally complete as my first observation is, as revealed from the Holy Bible of unified proportion, with all of its cosmic grandeur and universal consumption, yea, concluding the whole creation, I am shown by Jesus such a magnificence of the Father, which literally dwarfs that creation of the Heaven, the cosmos, and the universe, which they cannot receive at all. It is within and because of this that the world cannot know the Father who created them or who sent them to be created. That is, He sent forth the heavens, the cosmos, and the universes to be created, then He created them, and this was done without ascendance except for the angels.

Before we reveal the first observation of the greatest living work that believes can do and made possible only through Christ Jesus as the world should know because it is written in scripture, then afterward, the greatest revelation unknown to the whole world, the Father himself being revealed to the world the only way that they can know Him, through John 14:6. These words of Jesus having been proven true will reveal more about those powers, which operate within Jesus and His teachings. Have you considered how after He gave them power, He made an end of commanding His twelve disciples, and He then departed (Matt. 11:1)? Jesus departed by the transport method and standard set forth by this paper, conveyance.

It is easy to say that Jesus performed all the works promised by the prophets and that He fulfilled the works promised by others (Deut. 18:18, Isa. 61:1, Luke 4:21, and Isa. 35:5–6). Who are these that fly as a cloud and as the doves to their windows (Isa. 60:8)? Surely these fly as a cloud fly. Surely these fly as the dove to their windows. Surely these that fly, fly as a cloud as a cloud flies in the open space above the earth.

It appears from Matthew 8:1 that after His Sermon on the Mount, Jesus departed back to the mountain from the mount for prayer and giving of thanks before He came down from the mountain.

When you can command power the way Jesus did, nothing is impossible unto you, whether the world believes it or not. Every power that can be imagined by the human mind or heart was under the command of Jesus without interference or doubt. In fact, in Matthew 28:18, He realized and proclaimed after astounding both Heaven and hell after His resurrection from the dead and was not about to ascend into the heavens far above all principalities, power, might, and dominion without proclaiming; all power is given unto me in Heaven and in earth, and He is in perfect command of it all.

Now when Jesus gave the commandment to depart unto the other side (Matt. 8:18), surely the believer can understand the force behind His instruction in Mark 11:23; for verily I say unto you, that whosoever shall say unto this mountain, be thou removed and be cast into the sea, and shall not doubt in his heart but shall believe that those things which he saith shall come to pass; he shall have whatsoever he saith. He gave commandment to depart unto the other side. There was no doubt in His heart. He believed those things and people that He commanded, and He had whatsoever He commanded.

A question was asked by the apostles at sea, which has yet to be answered, at least to my knowledge. After euroclydon ravished the ship in which Jesus was aboard, asleep, and the disciples came to Him and awakened Him, saying, "Lord, save us. We perish" (Matt. 8:25). The question arose after Jesus admonished them with, "Why are ye fearful, O ye of little faith?" Then He arose and rebuked the winds and the sea, and there was a great calm. Euroclydon had been silenced, and there was a great calm. The most marvelous sight was to see Jesus rise up into the midst of the storm from off the ship and into the air and rebuke the winds and the sea from the air. Having consumed euroclydon, the men marveled, exclaiming, "What manner of man is this that even the winds and the sea obey Him?" The man that did it all is the manner of this man, and His care is that they perish not. See His words of rebuke in Mark 4:39 for joy in the appreciation of the word of God commanding the natural elements of nature. Compare Genesis 1:3 with Mark 4:39 and let the believer rejoice, and there was light, and in there was a great calm.

For those believers who desire evangelism with its gift and passion; euaggelion, meaning gospel or good news, is taken forth with the purpose of responding to God's grace through Christ Jesus, with not a single glimpse from church history or visible related evidence of such a powerful evangelistic spirit during Jesus's days. There is recorded evidence of works being performed in Jesus's day by those who were not among the holy apostles (Mark 9:38). John presented Jesus with eyewitness evidence that, "Master, we saw one casting out adversaries in Thy name." So here is undisputed evidence that works were being performed in Jesus's day by those who were not with the holy apostles. But let us take the most severe case of which most who attend church have not taught or heard.

There is no recorded case in the New Testament where the holy apostles reported the work of Jesus being done by one of the greatest acts of deliverance for evangelism (Mark 5:20), and in John 10:16, "about other sheep I have, which are not of this fold, must be examined also." This severe case for evangelism (Mark 5:1-20), is even more severe than the case with the apostle Paul being converted, as the act of Saul, who breathed out threats and slaughter against the disciples of the Lord (Acts 9:1). Saul had an obsession, which put the disciples of the Lord in peril. What condition could be worse for either Saul or for the disciples? We know through Luke's report in the book of the Acts of the Apostles that Saul was converted and became the first great evangelist, traveling as far as Rome after his baptism by Ananias at Damascus, where he, like John the Baptist, was also beheaded.

What worse condition could exist? According to Matthew 8:28, Mark 5:1, and Luke 8:26, Jesus and those who were with Him came over to the other side of the sea. No, neither He nor those with Him were conveyed at this time, but they were conveyed to the ship when He commanded in Matthew 8:18, and as shown in Matthew 8:23.

Those who attend church know quite well about a man with an unclean spirit dwelling among the tombs. When you read Mark 5:5, you read the saddened condition about him crying and cutting himself with stones. He was about to receive a translation for evangelism, of which no other scripture can match. When the casting out, the cleansing, and the transformation were complete, they that came to see Jesus and to see him that was possessed with the adversary and had legions, saw him sitting and clothed and was in his right mind (Mark 5:15). He was now ready to receive his commission for evangelism directly from Jesus (Mark 5:19). Note in Mark 5:17 where they began to pray him out of their coasts and also note Mark 5:20, the work of evangelism being broadcasted as a testimony to those who formerly knew him, of what the Lord Jesus had worked upon him.

Now read the great work of evangelism, which was done by someone other than those who besought Jesus to depart from their coasts. The acceptance and the effect can be seen upon His later return to Gennesaret (Matt. 14:34). The whole area is now converted and besought Him not to depart out of their coasts but that they might only touch the hem of His garment (Matt. 14:36). We can see further proof of the great works of evangelism in Mark 6:53. How was it that they knew Him (Mark 6:54)? As is the nature of Jesus, anything He does once, He can also do twice. If He walked on the sea once, He can also walk upon the sea twice.

In the application of the wisdom and works of the world of nature, whose wisdom and works are very vast per square inch at any given time, day or night, on land, on sea, or in her skies and are always active, how much of it do the believers see? How then can they know the fulfillment of these words of Jesus of Matthew 13:16: Blessed are your eyes, for they see. Or for your ears, for they hear, or even deeper, taste or smell? This is the fulfillment of their faculties through Him.

TRUE BELIEVERS OF THE TRUE WORKS

WE WILL NOW BRING the true believers of the true works of Christ Jesus beyond all works of the arising false Christ revealed by Jesus in Matthew 24:24. For there He prophesied that, "For there shall arise false christs and false prophets and shall show great signs and wonders; insomuch that if it were possible, they shall deceive the very elect."

Now why is it that these false christs and false prophets shall deceive the very elect? What possible kinds of great signs and wonders would they perform with the possibility and certainty of deceiving the very elect? No believer has transcended this prophesied time of Jesus to know why it is that these false christs and false prophets shall deceive the very elect nor have they considered why the very elect was so vulnerable in the first place to false christs and prophets performing such great signs and wonders to such a magnitude of deception. Furthermore, they have not considered the nature that cannot ever be deceived by false christs and prophets, false signs and wonders, or otherwise. That is the nature of the begotten. False christs and false prophets with their lying signs and wonders arise out of the world and their heavenly works and wonders are of great magnitude, insomuch that if it were possible, they shall deceive the very elect. Their deceptions are found in scripture, and the very elect is not the only begotten because of choice. But God would not allow His very elect to be deceived, not even if it were possible.

God has preserved with purpose the realm beyond all works of the false christs and prophets, seeing that heaven and earth are to pass away. Therefore, it does not matter how many or how great a magnitude their heavenly works shall be; they only arise to deceive themselves with the world to carry out His more brilliant plan, being greater than their works and deceptions.

That realm beyond Matthew 24:24, of which we are shown to be greater, is even greater than Matthew 24:29, which is also a realm beyond Matthew 24:24. In Matthew 24:29, when the sun and moon burn out and quantum gravity becomes unified among the stars, and the last test of the powers of the heavens prove them, it's not that realm that we indicate. This indicative realm, although greater than those before, is far less than that realm of the Father.

Now when the sun of the present solar system burns out, eliminating daylight and it's activities and the principle for lighting up the night sky becomes inoperative and also eliminating nightlife of the nocturnal sort, wherein both the photosynthesis and the lunar growth processes vanish, these could only result in a collapse of their natures and causing starvation and fear of the worse sort spoken by Jesus in Luke 21:25–26, such as men's hearts failing them for fear and for looking after those things, which are coming on earth. The heat from the sun does keep its solar system within its marginal temperature balance because of its fusion process. There cannot be any doubt whatsoever that He who made the sun, moon, and stars, and all of the other hosts of the heavens has so much more power than the creation themselves. When you can narrow such great power down from such cosmic proportions to that brilliant process of creating the complexity of the human brain, with its fourteen billion cells with their neurons configured and consigned with their electrical impulses and transfer that brilliance below that of subatomic processes, causing subatomic vibrations below one-hundred-billionth volt as precisely measured by a well-engineered volt calculating machine, there can be no doubt whatsoever that He who made such things and processes possess so much more power than His creation. These papers agree with scripture and the holy apostles that Jesus is their responsible factor and consistence.

We will now move to the greatest biblical work to ever be imagined, concealed behind the creation of the whole world. When God created the world, He designed that great work with the purpose of liberation. Many, the world over, claim to know God with no adequate proof of their claim with God at all. These papers do not take the Corinthians' view of those Corinthians of 2 Corinthians 13:3, who seek proof of God or Christ speaking through those making their claim to have that knowledge. But if their claims are true, and they are truly found to know God or Jesus himself, these papers only ask those claimants to share such wonder and discovery, brilliance and supreme attainment with us. First, let those claimants consider this: when the God that they claim to know becomes revealed to these papers, there is always undoubted evidence that any claimant can obtain this knowledge through reading and scripture.

Now for the evidence of the creation for the purpose of liberation, we begin when God created the world (Gen. 1:1) He created it through Christ Jesus, who was also there as we have already defined His works of protection at the first heated instance, and we say at the first heated instance because any activity that would erupt into dimensions to the size and magnitude of the present creation would generate massive thermal affects. If the believer would seek biblical evidence of the present creation rising up to great dimensions, let him or her seek the words of Jesus about the kingdom of Heaven starting out small but growing up massive (Matt. 13:31–32 and Mark 4:31–32).

The creation for the purpose of liberation was the intended design of the work. It is sufficient to observe this knowledge for this great work of creation only. Who can possess such a determinant mind to behold such vastness is not the limiting factor of the mind. The mind must be tuned to grasp such vast magnitudes when you also consider in-depth observations within the cosmos of deep space, time, and gravity, and are able to grasp also their limitations among their magnitudes evenly.

What manner of mind is required to understand the intricacies of the creation, to comprehend how the creation is engineered, how it is brought into being, how it is built, or can the creation be improved upon to make a better creation? These intricacies or perplexities are of no use to the true believers of the Lord Christ. Nor is the manner of the mind required to understand any of these things about the creation of the universe or cosmos. The mind that pursues the answers to these intricacies of the creation of the cosmos and universe could never comprehend the primary purpose for the creation of the cosmos and universe. There has not been found in scripture the proof that the witness and writer of Genesis 1:1 was also aware of the primary purpose for the creation of the heaven and earth or the cosmos and universe. Although he wrote with no doubt or reservation, in the beginning, God created the Heaven and the earth in the beginning of the bible. However, wisdom, speaking from her principal place, said, "When He prepared the heavens, I was there. When He set a compass upon the face of the depth (Prov. 8:27), this was a compass of darkness, according to Genesis 1:2. But even when He prepared the heavens in the very presence of wisdom and even though wisdom also witnessed God encompassing the face of the deep to implant darkness thereupon, which He also created (Isa. 45:7), the revelation of the purpose for these great works of creation are found, like the word of eternity, in only one place (Isa. 57:15), and that place is found in Romans 8:19, and it is to this end and purpose that we become sons of God, that we may achieve the primary purpose for the creation of the cosmos and universe.

When the sons of God come to the fullness of the time appointed by the Father, according to Galatians 4:1–7, then the purpose for the whole creation shall be brought to pass (Rom. 8:21). The whole creation shall be delivered from the bondage of corruption although it may appear as an ellipse surrounded by a cloud; it is not the surrounding cloud, which holds the creation in its bondage of corruption, into that glorious liberty of the children of God. Therefore, no one else, or anything else, matters except God and His children, to whom He will deliver the whole cosmic and universe creation. Herein lies the primary purpose for Genesis 1:1. In the beginning, God created the heaven and the earth for the inheritance of His children. But you may say, the heaven and the earth are to pass away. This is true according to both testaments; they shall (Isa. 51:6 and Matt. 24:35), but their expanse and their form is not their substance.

Would the reader, whether he is a true believer of the Lord Jesus or not, believe that there can be no greater work than this for this whole creation? What other works, even those greater works spoken by Jesus of John 14:12, or of those of Matthew 24:24, can there be left over to do? Amen!

We have seen some of those works performed by Jesus. John said in his writings that there are also many other things that Jesus did, that, if they should be written every one, I suppose that even the world itself could not contain the books that should be written (John 21:25). Some of these many other things, besides the recorded works that He did, we have revealed in minute portions. He appeared in another form unto two of them as they walked and went into the country (Mark 16:12). On this occasion, He may have appeared as a human orrery (a human mechanical model of the solar system) or of some other cosmic form. One thing is certain while He was in that form, whether eyes could behold Him or not (Luke 24:16), He did not use walking as a means of transporting himself. On other occasions, when He literally vanished out of their sight (Luke 24:31), or when He appeared out of thin air before the disciples (John 20:19), during these acts did Jesus use the floor to support His balance, as He came and stood in the midst of them.

If you consume the cosmos and the universe and all of the works of the cosmos and universe, then would they be dissolved within that consumption? There can be no doubt; consume the whole creation, and all of the works of the creation would be dissolved likewise.

THE TRUE AND LIVING GOD

WE NOW COME TO that realm of majesty, sovereignty, divinity, honor and dignity, love, integrity, thrones and multiples of thrones, mansions and a host of mansions, words and voices, lightning and thundering, magnificence and excellency. A life, where nothing shall be old with the more excellent way. It may be said that an eternal description may be rightly placed here, yet we are eons away from the fatherly source, whatsoever He may be or appear as. On one occasion of His heavenly visits, Enoch claimed to have seen the face of God, and he described it as an ineffable beauty burning with sparks of fire. Israel has claimed to see God face to face (Gen. 32:30). He appeared unto Abram (Gen. 17:1), and Moses was afraid to look upon God (Exod. 3:6). Adam and Eve hid themselves from the presence of God (Gen. 3:8). Moses brought the people out of the camp to meet with God (Exod. 19:17). The elders saw the God of Israel (Exod. 24:10). The prophet Isaiah saw the Lord (Isa. 6:1). The prophet Ezekiel saw visions of God (Ezek. 1:1), and the list continues.

In John 14:8, Philip saith unto Jesus, "Lord, show us the Father, and it sufficeth us." Nowhere within the history of the literature of the world, whether religious or otherwise, succinct with specific meaning and desire, been put in the form of a request to see the Father of all creations. Although in the mythologies there are gods who are fathers of lesser gods, history has proven them to be only mythological or an imaginary concoction from some creative mind. When you compare their works with those of the works of Jesus, there is no literal comparison at all.

Here Philip requested for the results of the magnitude of the exact yearning of Jesus himself, when He was suffice to deliberate upon this rock, I will build my church (Matt. 16:18). Here Philip, like Jesus, was looking for sufficiency, and as Jesus found his sufficiency from the Father (Matt. 18:17), Philip also found his sufficiency from the Father (John 14:9). The sufficiency of Jesus came after his desire to have his request fulfilled; flesh and blood hath not revealed it unto thee, but my Father, who is in Heaven, and as the result of Jesus's asking, the church rock emerged, giving Jesus sufficiency of soul. With this sufficiency of His soul comes the birth of a Father's liberty: I will give unto thee the keys of the kingdom of Heaven (Matt. 16:19). Now if Matthew 13:11 is true, because it is given unto you to know the mysteries of the kingdom of Heaven, and Matthew 13:19 is also true, I will give unto thee the keys of the kingdom of Heaven also; much if not all is about to be unlocked to be revealed of Heaven's mysteries, or at least the opportunity is present for their revelations. Out of the desire to behold the Father for the sufficiency of their souls, Philip requested to be shown the Father. After having heard the Father speak from Heaven (John 12:28) in direct response to Jesus's request, it would also be a simple request to ask to see the Father, especially since being told by Jesus after the revelation of the voice from Heaven that this voice came not because of me but for your sakes (John 12:30). Philip thought, if this voice came from Heaven at the request of him also and for our sake again, He can show us the Father to suffice us to the satisfying of our souls.

The greatest mystery never to be made known by the world is about to be revealed away from the flesh and blood of the world. The world cannot make it known, and it is not revealed through flesh and blood, according to scripture.

As it is documented and recorded in the scripture (Matt. 11:27), which claims, all things are delivered unto me of my Father, and no man knoweth the Son, but the Father; neither knoweth any man the Father, save the Son, and He to whomsoever the Son will reveal Him, and John 1:18 also testifies that no man hath seen God at any time, the only begotten Son, which is in the bosom of the Father, He hath declared Him, and John 6:46 asserts that not that any man hath see the Father, save He which is of God, He hath seen the Father. Therefore, access into this realm is solely through Jesus alone (2 Pet. 1:11).

The world with all of the mega brilliance of the arts, sciences, and the technologies cannot know of this realm because out of this realm came worlds and works as has already been proven by Jesus (John 15:24). If I had not done among them the works that no other man did, they had not had sin, worlds as distinct from this world as the works of Jesus is distinct from those of any man.

To compare the brilliance of some of those worlds with the mega brilliance of the present world, consider not the works of Jesus that He did, which no other man did in comparing creatures and their works to their worlds; neither consider biological agents present for a particular condition for life. But take observation from an abundant element found necessary not only for earthly life, which is found in great abundance within the very deepest confines of the cosmos and space. This abundant element, which is actually metallic, is hydrogen, a highly flammable gaseous element, the most abundant in the universe, easy to ignite on judgment day (Heb. 12:29). Seeing our God is a consuming fire, but when it is subjected to billions of atmospheres, it becomes transparent steel. Therefore, there are conditions along the scale for the most abundant element of the universe for other worlds and greater to exist. It is thought that three billion years along the scale when matter and energy is decoupled, there would be universal transparency.

It may appear difficult to the world to fathom the most abundant gas in the universe and which is so flammable, seeing God as a consuming fire, and knowing He created the universe, yet the universe has not yet been inflamed and burned. It may also seem difficult to digest how hundreds of thousands of suns remain inflamed in flammable abundant hydrogen or how supernovas explode and new stars and galaxies are born in fiery displays of power within the flammable and universal element of hydrogen. Yet God is a consuming fire who made both universe and hydrogen. Upon a closer examination, it would become clear to the believer of this.

From this realm, we can see the origin of the conception of the church, as well as the origin of the conception of all worlds and things. From here, we also understand the origin of the conception in Romans 8:21, wherein the creation itself after the fact of the truth shall be delivered from the bondage of corruption into the glorious liberty of the children of God.

There are worlds that not only reach the limitations of the present world but that extend even onward and beyond.

Sometimes, Jesus would gather up the fragments that would remain after a miracle and would send those fragments back into oblivion so that nothing would be lost. The impact of this oblivion will show among the apostles (John 17:12).

The observation of the origins of all concepts may be gathered from this general revelation found in Luke 10:22. All things that are delivered to me of my Father, and no man knoweth who the Son is but the Father, and who the Father is but the Son, and he to whom the Son will reveal Him.

Perhaps the believer, if not the reader, and it may be that the believer cannot read at all, because faith cometh by hearing (Rom. 10:17), can appreciate something of a broad concern maintained within God's focus and care about the hundreds of many millions of sparrows found throughout the new world, to help us broaden his horizon for acceptance of what is to come afterward, and which more than encompass the entire creation. In the new world, Central Asia, Africa, and North

America, there are many hundreds of many millions of the sparrow family. Jesus declared in Luke 12:6 that not one of them is forgotten before God. After all, they too must be fed daily.

Now to speak of that which encompasses creation, in comparison to other worlds and works, is of no great importance to anything greater. Not one little sparrow is forgotten before God, yet God can choose to forget that by which He pleases himself (Jer. 31:34). I will remember their sin no more. Total forgetfulness (Isa. 65:17). Therefore, it is of the will of the Creator to remember or to forget the transfer of the creation into that glorious liberty.

Jesus said in Luke 10:22: All things are delivered to me of my Father, while in Romans 8:21, the creation is delivered from its bondage of corruption also. Now if you were to compare Jesus's definition of all things to that with creation, then the creation itself with its cosmos would amount to about an atomic particle in space, as it is known.

These papers should ask that most concerned question of Jesus: how readeth thou? How readeth thou about such an atomic creation such as atomic cosmos, such an atomic universe?

THE SPIRIT OF TRUTH

ARMED WITH SUCH AN understanding, we now venture to comprehend those things of which the world cannot receive of the spirit of truth.

Blessed eyes are required to see the things shown them out of scripture. If by standing upon the shoulders of biblical giants, I have been made to see further, I would remind the reader and the believer of the Lord Jesus Christ of who these biblical giants are before the holy and divine eyes of God. These biblical giants upon whose shoulders I stand, looking intently upon what is seen from scripture, has both walked and has talked with the living God. They are the prophets and the apostles of scripture, according to Ephesians 2:20. Therefore, since we are built up already upon the foundation of the apostles and prophets with Christ in place, let us behold these wondrous things of God the Father through Christ Jesus, from their foundation. What do we see with our spiritual eyes from the scripture of which the world cannot receive?

The wisdom of God's godliness that is manifested away from the natural eyes of the world would be found hidden within mysteries to the eyes of the world, of those most learned in searching scripture, to have them revealed unto themselves, which God ordained before the world unto our glory. To venture into the depth of such wisdom of godliness away from the spirit of the world that we might know those things that are freely given to us by God through grace, we must first have the spirit, which is of God. Let us observe the disassociation of the world from the living God.

It seems as though this disassociation of the world has already been revealed even in the scriptures.

Unlike man in the world who prizes relics of ancient civilizations and histories, and it seems proper to say that, the world that was destroyed during the deluge of Noah is not likely to be remembered by its Creator. Under the circumstance and greater magnitude of what is about to be revealed by such a magnitude of mind and power and works of God can fully be comprehended with these words of God, the living Creator.

In Isaiah 65:17, how much power, how much space, how much matter, and the concept of space according to the absence of time (Rev. 10:6) and light (Rev. 22:15) seem not to belong either in this new creation in Isaiah 65:17. How much whatsoever is needed to construct such a new creation, even without space, time, and light? If the present creation is constructed with space, time, and light, consider this in Isaiah 65:17: the former, which include space, time, and light shall not be remembered in the creation of the new heavens and new earth, which would be a vast undertaking. But even greater still, they (space, time, and light) will not come into mind for remembrance nor usage for construction. Consider the unknown promise of Isaiah 65:18.

Look across the vastness of the deep cosmic universe and behold those reaches within the stretch of many billions of light years stretching out across space and time. In addition to creating the new heavens and a new earth, this former stretch of the deep cosmic universe shall not be remembered. How can something so vast hold so little importance that it would not be remembered nor will it come into mind?

Even if all things are delivered unto Jesus according to Luke 10:22, how would it be that Jesus himself could keep such vast things from the memory and mind of God? In these papers, it is accepted that only the mind of Christ Jesus has such a capacity and retention power so that the former cosmic universe shall not be remembered nor come into mind. The understanding opens doors to new dynamics beyond those of the world order.

It is proper to comprehend this lineage of thinking and understanding in lieu of greater works of obedience beyond those of worldly disobedience practiced by the world. There are some of you that walked according to the course of this world, according to the prince of the power of the air, and you know who he is and where in the world he now works (Eph. 2:2).

Lay away all worldly knowledge and let it cease, for the day of the Lord is at hand. It is the day for the edifying of the body of Christ. It is the time for the stature of the uninhabited fullness of Christ. It is of this uninhibited stature of the fullness of Christ that the manifestation in the highest order of the creation can adjust itself to, in order to prepare itself for deliverance from the bondage of corruption.

How can God be so merciful unto us to accept us as children of God? Who are we that we can be, or even could be, the children of God? Although you may not think your mind to be that of Christ, although you may not think your mind to capacitate the whole creation, if you would accept the power in John 1:12 to become the sons of God, even to them who believe in His name, and if you can accept the promise of Romans 8:21 that the creation (universe) itself also shall be delivered from the bondage of corruption into the glorious liberty of the children of God, you then ought to liberate yourself as a son of God so that He may cause you to liberate the universe from its bondage of corruption. This then is far greater than any earthly works of Christ Jesus, according to John 14:12.

May the spirit of grace and of truth be with you all in the name of the Father, and of His son Jesus, and of the Holy Ghost. Amen.

Golden Amen!

Part II

Sons and Daughters

Manifesting

For the Father's Glory

**Scriptural Proof and Benefits
of Sons and Daughters of
God the Father**

Isaiah 43:5   Fear not: for I am with thee: I will bring thy seed from the east, and gather thee from the west;

6   I will say to the north. Give up; and to the south, keep not back: bring My sons from afar, and My daughters from the ends of the earth;

7   Even every one that is called by My name: for I have created him for My glory, I have formed him; yea, I have made him.

CONTENTS

Introduction
-[113]-

The Era of the Holy Apostles
-[115]-

Higher Knowledge in the Holy Ghost
-[121]-

Excelsior My Children
-[123]-

Designs Fit for Heritage
-[130]-

Spirit
-[137]-

Great Heritage
-[140]-

Lights
-[145]-

INTRODUCTION

IN THE WISDOM OF the world, there is no desire to know God who created the heavens as our Father. In the history of the world, God, who fashioned the heavens, is looked upon with the mode of the servants' mentality. This servant mentality has caused the mind of the possessing mode to become spiritually blind to much higher attainments and callings ascribed in scripture. These much higher attainments and callings lie unanswered by the masses over the course of church history. How many major prophets of which we have not heard have daunted the world throughout church history? It also seems absent from history, those of the caliber of the holy apostles. We would not hesitate to accept an Agabus (Acts 11:27–29), who visited the church at Antioch and predicted a world famine, who also predicted Paul's encounter at Jerusalem (Acts 21:10–11), speaking by the Holy Ghost.

At the close of the era of the holy apostles, the higher attainments and callings of God the Father seemed to taper off from the church although the holy apostles speaking by the Holy Ghost revealed many high things from God, not to mention those very high things also mentioned by Jesus.

It would satisfy us if we would show some of these high things of scripture from the different apostles for the sake of the church and saints. There can be no doubt that God would not have you ignorant of His transforming knowledge, having you designed for a better and fitter world.

THE ERA OF THE HOLY APOSTLES

THE ERA OF THE holy apostles was very rich in things pertaining to those things of God in making those present desires to achieve higher callings and greater works by the transforming of their minds to greater and higher things of God. It was a time of enrichment and renewing of the old standard of farming, shepherding, fishing, boat making, masonry, carpentry, quarrying, military oddities, and a host of other civil endeavors to which the mind catered. The history leading up to the era of the holy apostles was vastly rich in the things of God from Old Testament scripts and writings. But most of those things, which were written by the holy prophets, were not written in favor of the uplifting of the mind of the people to whom they were sent to show those high and wonderful things of God. Even though He had promised to place them high above all the nations of the world and exclaiming that they of the world were as a drop of water in a bucket, even the man Moses had to go up to God, and God went up from Abraham. He came down to Adam and Eve in the garden, and He took Enoch and Elijah and Jesus skyward.

Please be settled in your mind that the cosmic bodies of the heavens have not varied much from their course nor contained capacities. In fact, not since the history of bible writing have they changed or been altered little. There are those who have displayed power over the heavens to the amazement of others, but they were in the will of God in these performances. There are those who have encountered angels, which performed feats under the will of God also.

At the close of the era of the holy apostles, the higher attainment and calling of God, the Father has tapered off from the church. The last great act among the holy apostles as it is recorded collectively among the Jewish apostles is not found of judgment but in glory and inheritance recorded by one who accompanied the apostle Paul (Acts 4:31). Again, they were all collectively filled with the Holy Ghost, and they spoke the word of God with boldness. They were all being filled again with the Holy Ghost through prayer and testimony of themselves, and Peter and John did bring to an end in scripture the last great act of God among the holy apostles. According to what is written about the presence of the Holy Ghost at this time, even according to the presence of the Holy Ghost in their first encounter (Acts 2:2–4), there seemed to be no room for higher callings of the Holy Ghost. However, examination of both accounts should be brought under the strictest sense of truth and power to ascertain whether there is room for the higher attainments and calling of God. There is proof of a greater spirit present during the advent of the Holy Ghost away from this lot and by the chief apostle Peter, himself. But great revelations from these two Holy Ghost advents should surface to cancel out ignorance of any kind and should bring to understanding written revelations during these advents of the Holy Ghost, revealing an accordance that is verbal among them here.

We will come to the greater spirit presence within an advent of the Holy Ghost under the anointing from the apostle Peter wherein you may judge what is written and revealed from scripture and truth.

In Acts 2:1, when the day of Pentecost has fully come, they were all with one accord in one place. How do you interpret "they were all with one accord in one place"? Usually the interpretation is translated that they were all with one accord in the upper room and that they were there when the day of Pentecost came. They had been there at the command of Jesus just moments before His ascent into heaven. In Acts 1:4–5, being assembled together with Jesus, He commanded them that they should not depart from Jerusalem but to wait for the promise of the Father, which ye have heard of me. For John truly baptized with water, but ye shall be baptized with the Holy Ghost not many days hence. And when the day of Pentecost came, here they are: all with one accord in one place.

But the question was asked, how do you interpret they were all with one accord in one place? The usual translation from the interpretation is that they were in the upper room, where they were all assembled in prayer and waiting for the Holy Ghost of promise. The church is correct in this interpretation of the place and in accordance of prayer in the upper room. But we can examine more closely the scripture at another place with the same praying and waiting group after having received the promise of the Holy Ghost in Acts 2:2–4, and also see an accord in grammar of one hundred and forty and five words, at which time God did not wink, nor did it take them by surprise as at the first appearance of the Holy Ghost. In this time, they came to one grammatical accord and place in prayer with all of them speaking the very same words in prayer. This was obviously the condition also for Acts 2:1. They all lifted up their voice to God with one accord, and when they had prayed, the place was shaken where they were assembled together and they were all filled with the Holy Ghost, and they spoke the word of God with boldness, and when every man heard them speak in his own language, they spoke the word of God with boldness in the streets of Jerusalem.

Now the search for higher attainment within these Holy Ghost advents continues forward. The one voice phenomena for masses is ancient in scripture (Exod. 24:3): All the words, which the Lord hath said will we do. This is the voice of the commitment of Israel to obedience to God. See Israel's one voice vow in Numbers 21:2, and the one voice in Deuteronomy 1:34. Only here in the book of Acts, the one voice is a prayer, all being also of one heart and of one soul.

This is indeed the last great act of the Holy Ghost recorded among the holy apostles, other than when they held council to form the decree for the gentile church at Antioch. The Holy Ghost was in attendance in the church at Antioch with the prophet Agabus, and through commissioning Paul and Barnabus for a short work among the Gentiles (Acts 13:2–4). The Holy Ghost said, "Separate me, Barnabus and Saul, for the work whereunto I have called them."

The experience in Acts 2:2–3 and Acts 4:31 was not recorded for Antioch in scripture, although something of great potential must have occurred there to cause so much church traffic to be drawn there. There is a wealth of encyclopedic knowledge of both Antiochs; where Christians were first named and gave no history of such an experienced magnitude. However, the Antioch that became Caesarea did record through the apostle Peter standing at Jerusalem (Acts 11:15) how that the Holy Ghost had affected the house of Cornelius just as it had done to the upper room, being the third time that the Holy Ghost had been recorded having a monumental affect in the scriptures. The Antioch three hundred miles north of Jerusalem is where the flow of church traffic was great among the apostles.

We will seek for greater and higher things of attainments of God simply because the holy apostles forecasted them in their epistles and gospels. If God can raise a dead man, surely He can also raise a living man. According to His promise, He raised unto Israel a savior, Jesus.

Before we end the era of the apostles in the search of higher attainments and godly experiences manifesting themselves as a living reality of evidence and proof of His glorious existence while yet alive, we have to examine another experience by an apostle of note at his conversion from persecutions. But as we approach this knowledge, we are shown how the holy apostles of ten moved about Jerusalem where Peter is in Antioch and in the temple searching with one accord how to glorify the Lord. How humble they are, having been conditioned by walking with Jesus and seeing His examples of humbleness, and of witnessing His tumultuous works of signs and wonders and miracles in defiance of nature, with Peter having walked upon water while with Jesus at sea, James and John having thought to call down fire from heaven in an attempt to please Jesus and Peter, and John having cured an impotent cripple from birth, and Thomas having to be shown proof after the resurrection. To behold them walking as a group in union even after their first and second experience of the Holy Ghost, all with one accord, is a magnificent wonder in itself to behold.

We now come to that apostle of note who also had an experience with the Lord Jesus in close proximity in the day of Pentecost. When we define close proximity, we mean that both were broad-based and godly experiences upon both groups. Both are confined to the same book of scripture with just a few chapters apart.

On the road to Damascus when the noonday sun has positioned itself so that its cone of light covers the earth with earthly images reflected sharply toward the apex of the sun's cone and illuminate the sky and brighten up the earth out over the peak, the brightness of the earth thunders and overshadows the brightness over the noonday sun.

You may wish to ask in today's inquisition of knowledge, since science, technology, and discoveries have advanced on all fronts, how could this have appeared in the noonday sky above the brightness of the sun when so very much knowledge of the sun, the Milky Way, and the cosmos is within the view and grasp of the click of a button? There are some that watch the constant arc of the sun within its solar flares and course and fusion tucked away with the planets southwestern within the Milky Way Galaxy and that have never heard of this Damascus phenomena so well reported on by such a noted apostle and the men who journeyed with him. This group of men was well advanced in knowledge. They were associated with the highest realm of religious knowledge of their day and had enough common sense to understand natural phenomena anywhere in the world.

It may not appear possible to those of the study of astronomy and astrophysics today how such a phenomena may occur anywhere within the Milky Way Galaxy with so many other suns abounding within the same galaxy. The answer to all such viewers and thinkers is that the Christian religion is not a religion of sight, sound, or thought, but the Christian religion is the religion of love, truth, faith, and in the belief in reality. All of the work of Christianity is not of mind, man, nor instrumentation, but all of the work of Christianity is under the control and governorship of Christ Jesus. Our faith came by hearing, and our hearing came by the work of our God who said that "ye can do nothing without me." Therefore, the light that appeared above the brightness of the noonday sun, which everyone saw, was consumed and translated into words of understanding for the heart, in order to change and convert the heart to Christianity for the purpose of salvation in saving the soul. You may view and study the Milky Way Galaxy, the Andromeda Galaxy, Galaxy NGC3198, and millions of other spiral galaxies within telescopic reach other than those that are shown from very deep space exploration, those galaxies whose numbers run into billions from five billion years ago to the big crunch vacuum and hole for all matter. These things you may view and study and even swim within them, but if you have not received by faith Jesus who made it all, whether you see it, explore it, walk upon it, or fly past it, you will never understand seeing a light and hearing a voice. We speak of a light above the brightness of any noonday sun and a voice unlike any other voice of history or life. This great difficulty is found in apprehending how God, the maker of all matter, space, and time, however much can come in the present form of man as Christ Jesus. But when you hear Jesus use correlated words like Ephphatha (Mark 7:34) for the heavens, the burden of acceptance comes easy.

HIGHER KNOWLEDGE IN THE HOLY GHOST

LET THE CHILDREN FIRST be filled, even in the higher knowledge in the Holy Ghost. What is the higher knowledge in the Holy Ghost? The apostle Paul called it the powers of the world to come. Scriptural proof and benefits of the sons and daughter of God in the powers of the world to come is not found in the promise of them from God the Father whom no man knoweth but the Son, but scriptural proof and the benefits of the sons and daughters of God in the powers of the world to come is found in our inheritance of them from God our Holy Father.

Have you not read that the bringing in of a better hope caused you to draw nigh unto God? Can you not hope to attain a better hope and a higher knowledge in the Holy Ghost to also draw you nearer to our God and Father of our Lord and Savior Jesus Christ who has duly made possible all things in Him for the glory of the majesty on high with worlds without end? We look to see higher knowledge in the precious Holy Ghost for His dear and holy sons and daughters. For within these things, far more evidence is obtained through love in our acquaintance of them with our Holy Father who is in heaven.

When we rise beyond all natural boundaries, which enclose and burden the mind and the spirits of all flesh, we are then ready to be loosed from world bondage and are then ready to be loosed from beneath the elements and the rudiments. Therefore, we are then able to obtain our physical communion with our loving and Holy Father through Christ who sendeth forth such wonderful knowledge for our acceptance into the beloved.

On the day of Pentecost, when the Holy Ghost fell upon the upper room to acquaint all with His comforting powers, giving all present their required speech and tongues for witnessing the glory of God for the testimony of His presence, which they did. Why was it and how is it that in this first outpouring of the promised Holy Ghost in Acts 1:5 by Jesus, we hear the apostle Peter speaking under the first anointing of the Holy Ghost and bearing witness in this anointing of this blessed Holy Ghost to the prophecy of the prophet Joel, the son of Pethuel, who lived here in the city of Jerusalem a few hundred years ago (Acts 2:17–21)?

Under this anointing of the presence of the Holy Ghost on this day of Pentecost, the apostle Peter (The Rock) proclaimed the arrival of the New Spirit promised by Joel (Joel means Yah is God) (Joel 2:28–32). But choose ye you sons and ye daughters of the living God of which of these ye shall take (Joel 2:28); I will pour out my spirit or in Acts 2:17, I will pour out of my spirit. Verily if I pour out my spirit, then ye have that which my spirit contains within itself. That is, ye have my whole spiritual containment. Thus, if I pour out of my spirit, then ye have that which is part of my spirit from within itself. In this outpouring of the spirit, ye receive those gifts and the anointing, which is comprised of the spirit from within the same. But if I pour out my spirit upon you, then ye become part of my spirit from without that I have poured upon and have placed upon you. Therefore, ye become gifts, and the anointing within the inheritance of the spirit itself being the same, is poured upon you.

EXCELSIOR MY CHILDREN

CRASHING THROUGH THE ROOF of the stars to be sheared off and away from them is your gifted freedom from world dominance, which shall be recompensed upon their own heads. Goodly and pleasant things await the sons and daughters of the living God. But before we explore designs fit only for such a heritage as ours through Christ Jesus, we will see the apostle Peter after his second experience with the Holy Ghost (Acts 2:4 and Acts 4:31), while he stood with the council of the other holy apostles and was reporting to those of the circumcision (Acts 11:2) about an astounding Holy Ghost revelation, which would cause him to witness his third encounter with the Paraclete.

It would do us well to know how the Holy Ghost first appeared after the promise of Jesus in Acts 1:4–5. Thus, wait for the promise of the Father, which ye have heard of me (Luke 24:49), for John truly baptized with water; but ye shall be baptized with the Holy Ghost not many days hence. It is very important that you should keep focus on Acts 1:5, which is the same as Luke 24:49, just moments before his ascent into heaven, which does not enter into the mouth of the anointed apostle Peter on the day of Pentecost. For further verification of the spirit being poured upon you and portions of the spirit being poured upon you, see Acts 2:16–17 for the action of the spirit for servants, and see Luke 4:18–19 for the six-fold ministry and anointing of the sons of God. In Joel 2:28: I will pour out my spirit; in Isaiah 61:1: The spirit of the Lord God is upon me; in Acts 2:17–18; I will pour out of my spirit, choose ye of which portion of the spirit of the Lord is greater in the anointing with power.

Now we will focus on the gracious anointing of the holy apostle Peter recounting his third encounter with the Holy Ghost in his defense before those of the circumcision at Jerusalem, especially since it has nothing to do with ye men of Israel. Except that the apostle Paul said that a grafting in of the Gentiles was necessary to reach them (Romans 11:17). But he even extended this grace of God unto the heathen (Galatians 3:8), even unto this ministry in Acts 13:41, behold, ye despisers, and wonder and perish, for I work a work in your days, a work which ye shall in no way believe, though a man declare it unto you. And through that grace, which was given unto us by the power of the living God through Christ Jesus, we have become the sons and daughters of the living God, grace for grace.

Now as Peter recounted the matter before those that were of the circumcision that contended with him, he recounted that the spirit bade me go with those sent from Caesarea, nothing doubting (Acts 11:12). After that, Cornelius recounted his experience in his own home to Peter (Acts 11:13–14), who had already had two previous encounters with the Paraclete (Acts 2:4 and Acts 4:31). He said, "And as I began to speak, the Holy Ghost fell on them as on us at the beginning." Now how did the Holy Ghost fall on them at the beginning? Let us return to Acts 2:1–4: and when the day of Pentecost has fully come, there they were all with one accord in one place and suddenly there came a sound from heaven like that of a rushing mighty wind. It filled all the house where they were sitting, and there appeared unto them cloven tongues like that of fire, and it sat upon each of them, and they were all filled with the Holy Ghost and began to speak with other tongues as the spirit gave them utterance. There were enough bodies in the upper room (120 bodies) to verify this same account to Luke who wrote of the eventful day. This was how the Holy Ghost fell on them at the beginning. The sudden sound from Heaven identified as a mighty rushing wind from heaven filled all the house where they were sitting; the appearance unto them cloven tongues like that of fire, and it sat upon each of them. This is how the appearance of the Holy Ghost on the day of Pentecost was recorded at the beginning, as it was promised by Jesus in Luke 24:49.

Therefore, since the apostle Peter was there and came under the anointing of the Holy Ghost at the beginning (Acts 2:1–5), and he was there also when it fell again (Acts 4:31), and since He also spoke under the anointing of the Holy Ghost, is he not also qualified to identify the entering in and works of the Holy Ghost? Yes. But our desire as sons and daughters of the living God and Father through Christ Jesus is to search through the Holy Scriptures that we may both fully live and fulfill them. We have the need to know that what Jesus says of the workings of the Holy Ghost will be borne witness through scripture, proving Him to be the truth of His workings as He said of it. He said, "And behold, I send the promise of my Father upon you, but tarry ye in the city of Jerusalem until ye be endued with power from on high." In obedience to this word of promise (Luke 24:49), it came to pass in Acts 2:2–4.

Therefore, we have known that what Jesus says of the workings of the Holy Ghost will be borne witness through scripture and proving Him to speak the truth of the workings of the Holy Ghost, as He said of it. When Jesus gave the apostles power in commissioning them in Matthew 10:1, Mark 3:15, and Luke 6:13, it was for the working among the earthly sort and kind. But when He gave them the promise of power in Luke 24:49, it was the promise of my Father upon you. When we apply this same principle for scripture, proving the truth of my Father, we have the need to know what our Father saith of the workings of His Holy Ghost that will be borne witness through His word, proving Him to be its truth working as He hath ordained it. What is there to be revealed of the workings of the Holy Ghost working with power from on High? There was suddenly a sound from heaven, like that of a rushing might wind. What occurred with this rushing sound from heaven? It filled all of the house where they were sitting.

How would you explain Acts 2:2 to a group of astronomers sitting and discussing a field of stars containing hundreds of millions of stars orbiting beyond some central galactic disc? We have already said that the works of God were works of faith and that no works or wonders of the deep cosmos shall save anyone. In fact, their own deep workings within the deep cosmos cannot save themselves nor the black holes within the midst of them.

The sun is aflame and on fire, but so are many of them with other orbiting bodies abounding with flames of fire leaping many millions of miles from their source. But if you notice on that day (Acts 2:3), there appeared unto them cloven tongues like that of fire. These many millions of flaming and orbiting bodies throwing their fires many millions of miles into cosmic space could not have been so specific as to direct flames particularly into this upper room, but if these flaming bodies of cosmic fires were able to direct such cosmic flames, those gathered in the upper room would not have been as fortunate as the bush with Moses nor of the three Hebrew boys with Daniel, especially since it set upon each of them.

We now come to the final point in the apostle Peter's defense against those that were circumcised. We have seen the effects of the Holy Ghost at the beginning, and we wish to know that what Jesus says of the precious Holy Ghost will prove truthful. The promise of the Father is manifested in Acts 2:2–4. The Holy Ghost came proving heavenly things, wind, fire, tongues, comfort, power from on high, but there was one thing that the Holy Ghost withheld on the day of Pentecost at Jerusalem, which was revealed at the home of Cornelius in Caesarea. For lack of a better understanding, maybe the Holy Ghost did not withhold anything since Psalm 84:11 saith: No good thing will He withhold from them that walk upright, and Proverbs 3:27 saith: Withhold not good from them to whom it is due, when it is in the power of thine hand to do it. And verily it was in the power of the hand of God and the promise to God to give out of the Holy Ghost on the day of Pentecost and to not withhold anything that was profitable to the works of God on earth from heaven.

We see the guideline of the Holy Ghost speaking as it is given Him to speak in Mark 13:11 and especially taking into account Luke 12:10, forbidding blasphemy against the Holy Ghost. We also see the guideline for the speaking of the truth by the Holy Ghost in John 16:13. Therefore, since we have such knowledge of the Holy Ghost from the Bible, which has come down through many generations of writers and printings, let us look at the words that are set before me spoken by Jesus in His descriptions of the workings of the Holy Ghost. Workings, which were not employed in the city of Jerusalem on the day of Pentecost by the holy apostles, even though he had heard these very words as Jesus was yet alive, before his crucifixion on Calvary, the workings of the Holy Ghost that did not surface on that Pentecost Day. This was said by Jesus even before His final moments at Bethany when He gave them the promise of Luke 24:49. Thus spoke Jesus, "But the Comforter, which is the Holy Ghost, whom the Father will send in my name, He shall teach you all things and bring all things to your remembrance, whatsoever I have said unto you" (John 14:26). If you can bear with me a little longer on this matter, here the apostle John records these words of Jesus speaking to them about the Comforter, which is the Holy Ghost, after He had broken bread with them at the last supper in the upper room. Thus, it is within the upper room that Jesus describes the workings of the Comforter (John 14:26). It is within this same upper room that the Holy Ghost descended on the day of Pentecost (Acts 2:1–4); therefore, when the Father sends Him here in this upper room in my name, He will bring all things to your remembrance, whatsoever I have said unto you.

In Acts 1:4–5, Luke 24:49, the verse 5 of Acts 1:4–5 would be excluded on the day of Pentecost in the upper room at Jerusalem, but verse 5 of Acts 1:4–5 would be included on the day that the Holy Ghost fell within the house of Cornelius in Caesarea, according to the apostle Peter in His defense among those that were of the circumcision (Acts 11:16). On the day when the Holy Ghost came in Jerusalem in Acts 2:2–4, the apostle Peter said in Acts 2:16, "But this is that which was spoken by the prophet Joel. The experience of the Holy Ghost had just occurred from the upper room here at Jerusalem" (Acts 2:2–4), but it was not promised to those of Crete or the Arabians or Romans, nor was it promised to any other people. But Luke 24:49, John 14:26, and Acts 1:4–5 were promised to the Jewish people; therefore, the apostle Peter referred to the prophet Joel on the day of Pentecost when he was called to fall under the anointing of the Holy Ghost for themselves and the Jewish people in general. There were dwelling on Jerusalem Jews, devout men out of every nation (of Jews) under Heaven (Acts 2:5). When we look at the Holy Ghost falling again for the purposed third time away from Jerusalem and the Jewish nation, we behold the outer foundation into the world of other nations, which was the cause of the apostle Peter's defense among those that were of the circumcision (Acts 11:3). Whereas the promise to the Jewish nation had come to pass of Jesus speaking to them about the Holy Ghost, He had earlier proclaimed in John 12:47: For I came not to judge the world, but to save the world. He came not to be partial to any of its nations existing the world over; therefore, into the world of other nations, the Holy Ghost had to come also. The apostle Peter would be the key for sending the Holy Ghost into other nations of the world also (Matt. 16:19).

As Abraham opened the door to the Jewish and Hebrew nation, Joel (Joel means Jah is God) closed that door on the day of Pentecost through the apostle Peter. But the apostle Peter would be the key for sending the Holy Ghost into other, yea, all nations of the world.

When the time had fully come for the dispensation for the Holy Ghost to enter into the world of other and all nations to disprove impartiality among the Jews, the apostle Peter was there also. When he began to speak in his own defense, he said, "And as I began to speak in the house of Cornelius in Caesarea, the Holy Ghost fell on them as at the beginning" (Acts 2:2–4), and then he said, "This is that which was spoken by the prophet Joel" (Acts 2:16). But when the precious Holy Ghost is to be sent into the world to other nations, those of you out there aware of Roman culture may wonder why a man of the ranks of Centurion and not of the higher caliber of emperor of the Roman empire, will receive such a gift into his household. Well first of all, Acts 10:2 reveals: A devout man and one that feared God with all his house, which gave much alms to the people and prayed to God always. Jesus said to pray always, and as was with the Pharisees with the Jewish people, it is very near impossible for those of high-ranking calibers to take note of God nor of the things of God (Luke 16:15). For that which is highly esteemed among men is abomination in the sight of God. And would the great God and our Father send forth His precious Comforter to those men of abomination? I wot not. Therefore, when the Holy Ghost fell upon the house of Cornelius in Caesarea, as on us at the beginning (Acts 2:2–4), Peter said, "Then remembered I the word of the Lord, how that he said, John indeed baptized with water, but ye shall be baptized with the Holy Ghost." In Jerusalem, among the Jews under the anointing of the same Holy Ghost, the apostle Peter spoke the words of the prophet Joel. But in the house of Cornelius, where Peter the apostle remembered the word of the Lord Jesus, brought to his remembrance by this same Holy Ghost (John 14:26), brought as on us at the beginning and since, suddenly there came a sound from heaven like that of a rushing mighty wind. Must we forget John 3:8: The wind bloweth where it listeth and thou hearest the sound thereof, but cannot tell whence it cometh, and whither it goeth, or at least in part? Only this wind did not blow where it pleased. This wind was sent by the Father and Son as the gateway to the nations of the world.

DESIGNS FIT FOR HERITAGE

THE EXPLORATION OF DESIGNS fit for heritage, you as sons and daughters of God can actually crash through the roof and top of the stars of heaven to be sheared off and away from them, but from the Bible's point of view in view of its prophecies against them is you ought to have the need to escape their fate and judgment from such a high setting in the heavens.

In the exploration of designs fit for heritage, let you, sons of God, and you, daughter of the same, behold the sun and the moon and the eleven stars, a very limited standard of heaven in Joseph's days (Gen. 37:9). Nevertheless, it is the same sun and the same in Genesis 1:16 of the former part of the verse existing in the present sky today. The eleven stars have grown to become, through gas and dust clouds strewn throughout the heavens to become many hundreds of billions within today's skies. As was with Joseph's coat, they are of many colors; therefore, the eleven star fields known within Israel's household have also increased among the masses now numbered within the cosmos, and fields upon fields are explored even further within the deeper cosmos and space. The Bible records that Joseph said, "Behold, the sun and the moon and the eleven stars made obeisance to me" (Gen. 37:9). How insignificant a part this revelation plays upon the mind of most without further exploring deeper meanings for the truth, even for and among these heavenly bodies known of Israel's household. Although of Israel's household the twelve tribes are there, it is the one mind of his household that the heavenly bodies are shown to pay obeisance, the soul that said to the heavenly bodies: Here am I.

How great the power that the mind must contain for heavenly bodies to make obeisance unto it. How great the power that the soul must commit to for their maker to surrender them over into it. The next branch after subduing the earth (Gen. 1:28) is the subduction of the heavens, and the next branch after the subduction of the heavens is the subduction of eternal life, which Jesus said in His revelation of the unlimited time it takes to know the only true God (John 17:3): And this life is eternal, that they might know thee, the only true God, and Jesus Christ (It is here that His begotten nature may be truly probed), whom thou hast sent. It takes an eternal life to know the only true God who made and set the heavenly bodies within skies. Therefore, it is with Him that Joseph found favor in this dream of obeisance upon the earth, in the open firmament of heaven. How many of you are there upon the earth in the open firmament of heaven that find favor with Him?

We have explored the design of the heavenly bodies fit for Joseph's heritage, and this would include how they function and operate according to today's discoveries. The sun still operates by fusion; the same moon has been walked upon, and fields of stars still orbit the Milky Way Galaxy in the firmament of the heaven.

There are those upon the earth, in the open firmament of heaven, even since the days of Jesus and today that still find favor with the only true God. We find this favor through spiritual gifts: tongues, praise, miracles, works, and love. To see this favor in operation upon the earth in the open firmament of Heaven in praise of Him is a wonder of love and favor to behold. As we come into the union of Genesis 1:31, when God saw everything that He had made, and behold, it was very good. Stay the course for this union is your heritage with Him who saw everything that He had made.

He was everything that He had made before He rested, and this included everything that He had made in its broadest reach and sense. Most do not include those things of the heavens: That their endurance is forever. To such ignorance, I refer you to Matthew 24:29 and Mark 13:25, wherein not only the stars shall fall from heaven but also the powers of the heavens shall be shaken. Let there be no doubt about the latter part (Luke 10:18): I beheld Satan as lightning fall from heaven, therefore none of their endurance is forever, though they be so high in the heavens, and this includes the fall of the prominent one of Revelations 9:1, who will receive the key of the bottomless pit. I had at one time thought to amuse myself of the whole world, especially to those of astronomy in viewing Abaddon whose name is Apollyon, as being the lucid angel responsible for all the black holes discovered at the center of very massive galaxies. But I thought of the world that neither the world nor I should worship adversaries. For it was God who made the heavens and that those who inhabit them should not be worshipped at all.

One of the most unique explorations of designs fit for heritage, having four degrees of freedom, is the gimbal shown to the prophet in vision: As I have vision of the wicked one being cast into eternal captivity into unquenchable fire. We turn not hierocracy into paleness by the revelation of the prophet's vision of God in the revelation of his gimbals or four degrees of freedom.

The great sky wheels, the great sky gimbals made to sparkle like chrysolite, which came to represent the very heavenly presence of God himself in his stationary sky, came to represent Jesus to the modern church.

In earlier writings that are now lost, great and infinite details were given unto me about these sky gimbals sparkling like chrysolite, which suggested that God manifested more than one method or that he manifested another way of creating hyperspace.

Upon very close examination of the sky wheels, luminous space stations far more futuristic and more moderately advanced over and above the earthly space station built like chrysolite sky gimbals or gyroscopes used for guidance, their whole nature is beyond the whole nature of mankind, which inhabit the earth. The great deimensions of their designs and likeness are of dimensions to which the human intellect cannot theorize nor confine to nature's laws of physics.

When you consider their degree of freedom in their general relativity to the New Jerusalem, their chrysolite brilliance and their lightening flashing transport, having such brilliant heights, there can be no comparison of anything that the human mind can imagine to stand within the shadow of such majestic heights and designs from such heavenly kinds.

Some say that these chrysolite wheels are the wheels of God's invisible chariot moving through the cosmic sky due to their great height, while others identify them with the chariots of the sun in their superstitious way of thinking, having not the knowledge of the works of the angels for the heavens themselves, which would one day be filled with clusters of fields of great masses of many descriptions and distances. Others identify them as the wheels of the throne of God on high. How vast a space is needed, how long a time is required and how splendid a beauty and majesty are wanted to construct the throne of God on high. Knowledge and understanding here is explosive in wonder, one of another, only God can be loved and praised, thanks to Jesus. Amen.

Now the ancient names of these sky wheels are called ofanims, which came from no root word. It was derived from the singular word for wheel (ofanim).

To behold the relative design of each of these wheels among each living creature with such a magnificence of design and power, with such brilliance of material as chrysolite is not to be compared in any wise to the operating force acting upon these sky gimbals (Ezek. 1:17).

Very close examination should be given to the likeness of these living creatures in passing among them having such knowledge and selection of material and having such wisdom in engineering such gimbals. In accordance with the normal but godly way of sharing his knowledge abroad through patterns, as was with Moses (Exo. 25:40) and David (Chro. 28:19), one can look and behold the conditions for patternmaking among that great spirit of nature, even as minute as quarks within protons and neutrons. It is through quark patterns that they are known and identified.

Now as for the likeness of these living creatures, their appearance was like burning coals of fire and like the appearance of lamps that went up and down among these living creatures, and the fire was bright and out of the fire went forth lightning (Ezek. 1:13–14). Behold, a great librarian of knowledge could be obtained here alone, but suffice it to say sons and daughters of the living God that I am not at liberty to ponder to record such. Nevertheless, Jesus has allowed me a little space to tarry to describe a little unto you of these living creatures of brilliance and speed of the vision of God.

When the sun is looked upon, being massive in hydrogen and helium, the tumultuous burning resembles a burning coal of fire. The waste thrown off is like the appearance of lamps, as some waste escapes as matter, heat, and radiation with enough force to free it from the sun's gravity into thousands of miles into space, while some returns to the surface of the sun as fuel to continue the fusion process of changing hydrogen into helium or carbon. Having a filter over lenses has revealed these far-reaching processes even to all stars having nuclear reactions within themselves.

According to the definition given to these living creatures by the world system, they are the seraphim because seraphim means the burning ones, and their definition also means devotional burning in their worship to God.

The appearance of the wheels and their work, unlike the faces, the wings, their mode of travel, their likeness, the velocity of the living creatures was unto the color of a beryl although beryl is a translucent glassy mineral with very many aerospace properties beyond such aerospace dynamics in the world of the spirit unto which these chrysolite wheels are subjected. Neither could these aerospace wheels be radio galaxies spinning in their upward surge and vastness among thousands.

The dynamics of these gimbals or gyroscopic-like wheels (a wheel in the middle of a wheel) (Ezek. 1:16) is that they had rings so high that they were dreadful, and you should be reminded of the rings of the planet Saturn of ice and moons, but not lodge therein because everything has the signature of the atom with the nucleus at its center, a wheel in the middle (a nucleus, a planet, an axle, a universe, a creation) of a wheel (Ezek. 1:16). The living creature sent knowledge of one of the wheels upon the earth (Ezek. 1:15).

Let us take the creation higher up into its existence and let all the world rejoice at being lifted up as sons and daughters of the living God. Can you envision wheels with their rings so high that they were dreadful, even being full of eyes round about them (Ezek. 1:18), moving with the velocity of a flash of lightning? (Ezek. 1:14, 1:17, and 1:19). Those having the mind of Christ as sons of men would understand Ezekiel 1:19–20, and verse 21 would reveal the general relativity among them both. For the spirit of the living creature was in the wheels. Who is the spirit of the living creature identified in verses 20 and 21? This spirit that has such awesome attracting and gigantic power over wheels with rings so high that they were dreadful? The rings of the wheels even as high as they are, must come under the power of this living creature.

If there be any world doubt as to the identity of this living creature with such awesome, high and quickening power and control, both upon the sky wheels and also upon himself, consider the heads of the living creature having many crowns in Revelations 19:12 and consider also the first part of Hebrews 4:12. Now you may consider Ezekiel 1:22. Like great megalantic clouds stretched out along the remote edges of the high cosmos like vast cosmic areas of radio galaxies stretched out throughout hyperspace, is the likeness of the firmament (as of that firmament prophesied in Genesis 1:6 upon the heads of the living creature, and it was the color of the terrible crystal, stretched forth over their heads above (Ezek. 1:18). But under the firmament were their wings straight (Ezek. 1:23). Do not forget that all matter has the atomic signature including the gyroscopic elements.

SPIRIT

GOD IS A SPIRIT, and they who worship Him must worship Him in spirit and truth.

There are those who worship spirit without an attempt at testing any spirit for God's signature and seal. The testing for the spirit is given in the words of 1 John 4:2, whereby you know the spirit of God, every spirit that confesseth that Jesus Christ has come in the flesh is of God. How many of you have actually heard this confession of the spirit that Jesus Christ has come in the flesh to prove that it was of God?

God is a spirit (John 4:24), and this confession of the spirit is acknowledged to be of God who is a true spirit. This confessing spirit, confessing that Jesus Christ has come in the flesh is of God. This acknowledging spirit is of God who is a spirit. He is a spirit that has an acknowledging confession that confesses that Jesus Christ has come in the flesh. Hereby know ye the spirit of God. You have heard that God is a spirit, but have you known that God is a spirit?

The wind bloweth were it listeth and thou hearest the sound thereof, but canst not tell whence it cometh and whither it goeth (John 3:8). Except a man be born of water and of the spirit, he cannot enter into the kingdom of spirit. He must be born of the water of the spirit and not of the water of the world, but of the living water of the spirit of life, which giveth life.

Every spirit, which is born of God, is manifested as the token of the wind. Before Jesus came in the flesh, flesh could not tell from whence it cometh and whither it goeth. Thanks be to God that Jesus came in the flesh and to have made these things known unto the church.

The spirit of life, which giveth life, is within Christ Jesus and those, which standeth and heareth Him rejoiceth greatly because of the bridegroom's voice. Amen.

Everyone that is born of the spirit is spirit; and of this, there can be no doubt. And the spirit testify of itself and searcheth all deep things of itself. It may do some well to know that the spirit was created, according to Isaiah 57:16: For the spirit (Ruach-Pneuma) should fail before me, and the souls, which I have made. Both spirit and soul should fail in their immortal substance before the high and lofty one that inhabiteth eternity, whose name is holy (Isa. 57:15): The Lord that created the heavens (Isa. 45:18), which saith: Behold, I create new heavens (Isa. 65:17). Those of you who become sons and daughters through John 1:12 by His power shall understand these things by John 3:31. He that cometh from heaven is above all, and for those of you that look for distinction, see John 17:14: Because they are not of the world, even as I am not of the world (His sonship disciples). Therefore, your spirit, His spirit is not from beneath (John 8:23).

A most staggering revelation, even more amazing than the astrophysical activities of the nuclear reactions at work and on display within massive radio galaxies, is that all of those works recorded of the gospels, of Jesus upon the earth, even though they defied both natural laws and laws of physics, they were all merely done in the capacity of the Son of Man and not in the divine capacity of the Son of God. He that believeth in me, the works that I do shall he do also (John 14:12) the works of the Son of Man. But in the spirit, greater works than these shall he do, the works of the Son of God. The greater works of the Son of God with promise and having received the power in John 1:12 to do the works of the Son of Man, you now through the spirit and his word received the promise of the greater works of the Son of God. Amen. Son of Man: earthly. Son of God: heavenly. Brethren, behold what manner of spirit given of God to him whom he sent to speak, and John bore record, saying, I saw the spirit descending from Heaven like a dove, and it abode upon Him. And I knew Him not, but he that sent me to baptize with water, the same said unto me, upon whom thou shalt see the spirit descending and remaining on Him, the same is He which baptizeth with the Holy Ghost (John 1:32–33).

John was also given the spirit to see the spirit, even in form, having taken on the form of a dove as he descended upon Jesus according to that promise made unto him. Having the spirit to observe the spirit as the spirit is sent into form, and having the spirit to observe the spirit as the spirit is sent out of that form is the manner of spirit given of God because giveth not God the spirit of measure unto him. For he whom God hath sent speaketh the words of God. And this also is without measure. John said, "And I saw, and bear record that this is the Son of God." Have you borne record and witnessed?

GREAT HERITAGE

JESUS, BEING MADE SO much better than angels from any rank and hierarchy of untold billions of them as he hath by inheritance obtained a more excellent name than they, hath made possible to man an entrance beyond world belief and acceptance.

The last order for the world was the setting up of the apostles, who were made a spectacle unto the world, angels and to men (1 Cor. 4:9). But no one has considered why spectacles were put in the order of men over angels and not angels over men, as is the world view. This was not a slip of the pen of the apostle, whose writing is flowing from a perfect spirit. In this verse, the apostle expresses what he thinks to be the order from God for exploits, from the last class of men upon the earth. In his thinking, this way he may appear to be right. But the order of the latter part of the verse: For we are made a spectacle unto the world, and to angels, and to men: God, hath set forth with purpose. The same purpose, which sparked the desire of the angels reported on by the apostle in his first epistle general (1 Pet. 1:12), which came with the promised Holy Ghost sent down from heaven. The myriads of hierarchy of angels were there in Heaven when the blessed Holy Ghost was sent down from heaven passed the angels from the throne of God on high. The order of the spectacle therefore of 1 Corinthians 4:9: a spectacle unto the world, angels, and to men was no mere writer's error. For God had in mind a purpose, and that purpose was for men to use his power to become what angels cannot become though they (men) may have angelic spirits (Heb. 1:14), and that is because angels cannot become sons of the living God. This is why men were placed beyond the order of the angels (John 1:12). You verily cannot actually know that Jesus is the Son of God, if you do not yourself become a son of God, having this witness within yourself.

Now that you understand why this order and purpose came to be set forth in 1 Corinthians 4:9, and we have been shown that the act performed at the gate of the temple which is called Beautiful (Acts 3:1–6) has played a divisive role in the mind of the apostle Peter, bless his spirit. We now turn to the Old Testament book of Job for an equally important point of observation concerning the sons of God. In Job 1:6, we read: Now there was a day when the sons of God came to present themselves before the Lord, and the enemy also came among them. It is obvious that this enemy is not of the sons of God and that he does not belong among such an elite and divine group who did not take notice of him at all because he is an offense to them. The Lord also would not have his dastardly attention drawn toward His sons at all that are sealed. The Father therefore immediately diverted the attention of the enemy away from His sons whom He protects, unto the consideration of Job (Job 1:8). In other words: I will not allow you to consider my sons, but you may consider my servant Job of the earth. And thus, the enemy went away to consider Job and the sons of Job. You be the judge as to which is more important to the Lord, His sons or His servant Job.

A great heritage must come with a great understanding. And the greatest heritage must come with the greatest understanding. The greatest understanding of the sons of God is what we are to inherit by lot but without measure from the Father.

If I tell you of heavenly heritages, would you receive them? There are vast differences between heavenly heritages and heavenly things. Those things, which are heavenly, are in part already created, whereas those heavenly heritages may come nowhere within the confines nor dimensions of the present heavens. You would not be a wise son or daughter of our living Father on high should you expect anything whatsoever of the present and perishable heavens although they, of late, render up very many of their works from both cosmic and hyperspace. But this is because of the fine-tuning of instrumentation and the advanced knowledge of space travel. But do not forget that any cosmic or astrophysical discovery or activities of late were already, or already is, in the growth process and operation of the heavens, even on the forefront of all major astrophysical discoveries to come. As for the magnitudes for any major cosmic discoveries of the present heavens, or even within them themselves, eternity stands far, far away from all laws of astrophysics governing the laws of the present heavens. Even the astrophysical laws governing quantum form beyond the horizon and singularity of astrophysical black holes reject present laws of physics requiring new laws of physics used to explain them, wherein those in present use in astrophysical activities would be a welcoming heritage for groups of astrophysicists exploring the wares within the present heavens.

These new laws of physics would first have to explain away in theoretical satisfaction the old theoretical laws of nature and astrophysical laws of the universe, which have awakened the mind of physics to the theoretical laws governing the universe and its activities, a task which none of the patriarchs knew of the Old Testament. The prophets with great insight into the laws of physics, although their description of these things were not specified, had no fault in and of themselves; the fault was in the ignorance of the masses. This fault existed until the time of Jesus. For anyone having seen the maker of all things, how could they not desire from him to have the knowledge of all things?

Although it is known that man is composed of ironically thirty-three elements, what man is there standing before his God and Creator that would not have asked, Lord how madest thou me? We should have the desire to fathom all of creation. Isaiah 55:6: Seek you the

Lord while He may be found, call ye upon Him while He is near, should have been the resolve for every man in general, even in this priori (Matt. 6:33): But seek ye first the kingdom of God and His righteousness. This manly resolve and priori ought not to have been and both should have naturally occurred generally and arrayed with glory. Of course, this would mean that if the present heavens are still under godly construction as astrophysicists think that they are with the vast astrophysical discoveries emanating daily from vast solar masses of black holes, the vast explosions from supernovas, neutron stars, vast cosmic explosions for great radio galaxies, the rushing away of untold numbers of outer galactic clusters, quasars of monumental size and speed, observations of the very fabrics of space itself being torn apart and dissolved, some into oblivion, and some into translation. Untold registers of radio waves from invisible and undiscovered sources sweeping the cosmos and hyperspace, discovering many astrophysical reasons for translations into and out of many dimensional universes, if the present heavens in these things (having vast space bubbles light years in diameter fizzing like sparkling water rising to a surface) are still under godly construction of these astrophysical activities, then man would also be proven incomplete.

He could never completely know God, who created or who incompletely created these astrophysical things with their activities. The truth is speaking another revelation. In Genesis 2:1, it is scripturally revealed that: Thus the heavens (the astrophysical cosmos) and the earth were finished and all the host of them. Therefore, since they were finished and all the host of them, anything found or discovered of them is nothing more than internal construction and activities of their already finished creation by Him who is the possessor of them (Gen. 14:19) who is the most high God. As God, He has dominion over them and over all of their astrophysical activities, whether yet discovered or not discovered, and however far away, however massive, or however explosive anything thereof might be: they were the decry of Jesus (John

19:30). It is finished. Thus, the heavens and the earth of Genesis 1:1 were finished, and all the host of them. In other words, the Big Bang is finished, and all that is seen and detected are astrophysical activities exploiting themselves among the already finished astrophysical elements within astrophysical spaces. Everything that may ever be found or discovered in or among the heavens and all the host of them are all part of a finished creation or a part of an unfinished astrophysical activity or of an unfinished astrophysical process. These are the generations of the heavens and of the earth when they were created in the day that the Lord God made the earth and the heavens.

LIGHTS

THE KNOWLEDGE OF GOD is almost unbearable in weight and mental excellence, O ye sons and daughters of the living God, whose heritage far exceeds any earthly heritage.

In the day that the Lord God made the earth and the heavens (Gen. 1:1), who was there in to witness such an arriving moment of the first splendor of godliness? The spirit of wisdom makes such claims in Proverbs 8:22, 23, and 27. When He prepared the heavens, I was there, wisdom proclaims. This was before the day that they were created. In the day that the Lord God made the earth and the heavens, this was to become that arriving moment of the first splendor of godliness for the world in the day (the very day) that the Lord God actually made the earth and heavens.

In Genesis 1:3, we read: And God said, let there be light (singularity), and there was light (singularity). As we know, it is not written for any other creation that God said: Let there be light also. If we look at light in its greatest sense of singularity, then the universe and its creation is far greater than the human mind can theorize, always bending the paths of light rays toward each other as a whole photon of light. This is revealed in lieu of Luke 16:8: for the children of this world are in their generation, wiser, than the children of light. This is because the children of this world have traced the natural light from its beginning through graphs and cones and have beheld density of matter to light, the intensity of light to the density of matter, the opaque energy of light to matter and gravity, the observation of the bending effect of light to other objects, the observation of the age and velocity of light, the observation of light variations within or near different fields measuring conditions, intensities, and light formations so that light has become the doctrine of their everyday source and instrument, even for instrument making and experimentation.

Truly the children of this world have generated more works through the doctrine of light than the children of light themselves. But is this not because of the ignorance of these children of light? After all, wisdom is justified of all her children (Matt. 11:19 and Luke 7:35). If wisdom can be justified of all her children as an agent called alongside God, who is greater than wisdom? How is it that the lesser children can justify the lesser, while the greater children do not, as they are far greater than both? All of the children of wisdom and all of the children of the world cannot, even in their generation, justify, yea, even glorify Him who is greater than all.

It would best do all the children of light to know that which Jesus taught on light. It may be that because this teaching of Jesus is not found in the gospels that the children have not taken firm hold on this revealing doctrine of light spoken by Him.

In 1 John 1:5, the apostle John who walked with Jesus, having been called by Him (Matt. 4:21 and Mark 1:19), revealed in this epistle the core of the message that they heard Jesus declare unto them and which He declared unto the church. This then is the message that we have heard of Him and declare unto you: that God is light, and in Him is no darkness at all. How is it that Jesus sees God as light? The answer to how Jesus sees God as light would fill a great many voids with knowledge. To speak words of spirit and life (John 6:63) that God is light is the perfect combination (spirit, life, and light) for eternal salvation.

If wisdom is justified of all her children, which is the lesser: ought not Jesus to have come to justify light? The answer in the affirmative is found in John 13:46: I am come a light into the world, that whosoever believeth on me should not abide in darkness. The whole world is overlaid in gross darkness.

There is little wonder that the children of the world in their generation are wiser than the children of light or that wisdom is justified of all her children, understanding the declaration of who light is and of where wisdom was with him before He spoke (Gen. 1:3).

Of all the sophisticated instrumentation, gadgets, measurements, and compositions that the children of this world have learned of light, in their many experimentations both far and near, even recording and theorizing its first instance at the Big Bang singularity and pluralizing other singularities of the same doctrinal system of light singularity. Are there other realms of light to ponder? Yes.

Let the whole world and the nations of it be aware of this one thing that within the abiding of anything, it is Jesus, the precious Son of the Living God, that has made any and all things possible, whether it be this world or any other things. Why would Jesus teach and declare that God is light? This question is answered with purpose in 1 John 1:7: But if we walk in the light, as He (Jesus) is in the light (God), we have fellowship (brotherhood) with one another. Therefore, if you have brotherhood with Christ Jesus in God, and you walk as He is in the light and radiance, from such a walk as He is in God, there would not be a cause for the children of the world in whatsoever they generate from the spectral doctrine of light to be wiser in their generation at all (Genesis 1:1). In the beginning, God (Light – 1 John 1:5) created the heavens and the earth. Fellowship on and with one another would be generated both in, from, and within the beginning when He created Heaven. We walk in the light as He is in the light. Amen.

If you look at the principal generations of the children of the world in their generation of works, the principal generations of all their works are founded and set up fundamentally from some earthly force or matter. If they are fundamentally founded and are set up from some earthly force or matter, then there must be principles and laws by which they operate. These principles and laws by which they operate are coerced by laws of nature, and being coerced by laws of nature, they are bound by laws of physics. Being bound by laws of physics, they are consigned to a frame of reference, and they must always be found fundamentally true in experimentation, setting out to prove or to disprove their worth.

In generations of works not belonging to the children of this world (such as the works of the children of light, which should be wiser generations of works than those of the world and its children's works), and we mean the works of the children of the world in its most advanced state of knowledge and translation of knowledge within advanced and sophisticated fields of technology today or in today's societies, you only need to observe what such works would reap for whose glory: for the Father or for the world? In John 10:38 Jesus said, "Believe the works that ye may know and believe. For many good works have I shown you from my Father" (John 10:32). Not one of the world's sophistications could be so advanced enough in neither wisdom nor technologies to draw near to match those works of Jesus in His many good works. Compare a system of computers with Jesus walking on water.

If any man walk in the day, he stumbleth not because he sees the light of this world. But if a man walk in the night, he stumbleth because there is no light in him (John 11:9–10). The light of this world and the light in Him is the difference.

What if there were vast worlds of other lights, worlds not having ordinary radiations of light as propagated throughout the space of the universe? It is true that the children of this world have found and applied an ancient purpose for light written in the holy scripture in Genesis 1:14. If the truth be rightly divided brethren of God, He gave a series of purposes for light in Genesis 1:14. As we read and rightly divide Genesis 1:14 to seek out this series of purposes assigned to light, let us rightly divide some of the ancient godly assigned purposes given in scripture for light.

In Genesis 1:14, God began to assign positions and purposes both to light and for light, as well as their magnitudes as light. And God said, let there be lights (magnitudes and intensities) in the firmament (positioned higher) of the heaven (positioned lower) to divide (the first purpose) the day from the night; and let them be for signs (higher and theoretical purposes) and for seasons (higher purposes for higher measurements) and for days (lower purposes for lower measurements) and years (to be used for measuring and measurements in light years), to measure distances throughout space. Should we venture even farther back into the primary purpose for light at the beginning of the creation (Gen. 1:3) when darkness was upon the face of the deep? Apparently there was a need and primary purpose for light because what had been accrued in darkness, as those works, which the Egyptians duplicated with Moses in the land of Egypt, had to be made manifest through light reflections and works. All things that are reproved are made manifest by the light (Eph. 5:13). O ye sons and daughters, remember the identity and the illustrations given by Jesus for you in the writings of the apostles (Matt. 5:13–16), Ye are the light of the world. A city that is set on a hill cannot be hid. This is your illustration. Remember also the purpose for the Comforter in John 16:7–11. When He comes, He will reprove the world.

A grand and panoramic spiritual view would suffice for those who are in Him in love and that have His words abiding deeply within themselves, who has accepted the call in John 1:12 and have become sons and daughters without rebuke and have beheld what manner of love in 1 John 3:1–3.

To close this book and chapter of light, I say this book of light for His sons and daughters because the book called the *Zohar* among Jewish mystics is also called the *Book of Light*. But of this book, take note that every good gift and every perfect gift is from above; and cometh down from our Father of lights, with whom is no variableness, neither show of turning (James 1:17). We are sons and daughters of His own will by the word of truth made possible through Christ Jesus, His preeminent, who only giveth immortality and dwelling in the light which no man can approach therein, whom no man hath seen nor can see.

To Him be honor and power everlasting. Amen. I love you. Golden Amen!

Thus ends these Jesus papers.

Printed in Great Britain
by Amazon